Effective Multi-Agency Partnerships

Putting Every Child Matters into Practice

Effective Multi-Agency Partnerships

Putting Every Child Matters into Practice

Rita Cheminais

Los Angeles • London • New Delhi • Singapore • Washington DC

© Rita Cheminais 2009

First published 2009
Reprinted 2013

362.7

SAGE Publications Ltd
1 Oliver's Yard
55 City Road
London EC1Y 1SP

SAGE Publications Inc.
2455 Teller Road
Thousand Oaks, California 91320

SAGE Publications India Pvt Ltd
B 1/I 1 Mohan Cooperative Industrial Area
Mathura Road
New Delhi 110 044

SAGE Publications Asia-Pacific Pte Ltd
3 Church Street
#10-04 Samsung Hub
Singapore 049483

Library of Congress Control Number: 2008931580

British Library Cataloguing in Publication data

A catalogue record for this book is available from the British Library

ISBN 978-1-84860-138-3
ISBN 978-1-84860-139-0 (pbk)

Typeset by C&M Digitals (P) Ltd, Chennai, India
Printed in Great Britain by Bell & Bain Ltd, Glasgow
Printed on paper from sustainable resources

MIX
Paper from
responsible sources
FSC® C007785
www.fsc.org

Contents

About the author

Rita Cheminais is a leading expert in the fields of inclusion, Every Child Matters and special educational needs (SEN) in primary, secondary and special schools, and in local authority Children's Services.

With a background as a teacher, a SEN Co-ordinator, an Office for Standards in Education (OFSTED) Inspector, a Senior Adviser and a School Improvement Partner, Rita has over thirty years of practical experience.

She is a prolific writer and respected author of journal articles and books in the field of inclusion, Every Child Matters and SEN. Rita speaks regularly at national conferences and was one of the three 'Ask the Experts' participating in the Becta National Grid for Learning (NGfL) live online national inclusion conference in 2003. She provided consultancy on inclusion to the national Rolls-Royce Science Prize initiative for schools in 2004.

Currently, Rita is an independent education consultant with Every Child Matters (ECM) Solutions. She provides keynote presentations at conferences as well as offering support and consultancy to educational settings wishing to achieve the Every Child Matters Standards Award.

email: admin@ecm-solutions.org.uk
web: www.ecm-solutions.org.uk

Dedication

I would like to dedicate this book to my late mother, Joan Cheminais, who during the last months of her life continued to ask me about the progress of my writing. She never failed to support, encourage and inspire me throughout my working career. Life will never be the same without her, and whatever the future may bring, I am truly indebted to my mother for giving me the benefit of her infinite wisdom over the many happy years we spent together.

Acknowledgements

I wish to acknowledge the appreciation and the positive interactions I have experienced with the many audiences I have spoken to across the country, and within Tameside. The interaction and discussions with school leaders and managers, teachers, teaching assistants, governors, parents, front-line practitioners and professionals from local authority Children's Services have helped to shape my thinking during the writing of this book.

Many thanks also go to the following for allowing the reproduction of materials with kind permission:

Anne McMurray

Cambridgeshire County Council

Centre for British Teachers (CfBT)

Continyou (Table 2.4)

David Wilcox

DCSF

Educe Ltd

Phil Lovegrove

Lilani Wijayatilake

National Foundation for Education Research (NfER)

Times Educational Supplement (TES)

I am eternally grateful to all those friends and colleagues who I have worked with, for their continued interest, enthusiasm and encouragement in keeping me focused to write practical books on Every Child Matters for busy practitioners.

Last but not least, I would like to thank Jude Bowen, Senior Commissioning Editor and Amy Jarrold, Editorial Assistant at Sage Publications, for their support, advice and guidance in making my initial book proposal become a reality.

Introduction

This book is for all those senior leaders and managers, teaching and support staff, including multi-agency front-line practitioners from health, social care, education and voluntary and community sector (VCS) organizations, working in partnership within a range of educational settings and children's centres, to improve the Every Child Matters outcomes for children and young people. The key message of this book is that multi-agency partnership working will not be effective unless it is based on trust and mutual respect between each children's workforce practitioner, who is clear about their role and the value they add in improving children's well-being.

'Partnership' as a term means different things to different people, working in different contexts. In relation to multi-agency partnership working it is about different services joining together in order to prevent problems from occurring in the first place.

Of all the different professional working partnerships in existence, multi-agency partnership working is the most complex and challenging process to manage and co-ordinate, within an educational setting, as evident in this comment by a full service extended schools (FSES) co-ordinator: 'It's hard work. It is constantly talking, emailing, communicating with them, being positive, keeping them involved, making sure they're happy, that they've got their office space, and their time slot. It's time consuming' (CfBT, 2007: 93).

The dynamics and outcomes of multi-agency partnerships can be unpredictable, unique and sometimes unknown, due to them being organic and continually evolving. Educational organizations from early years settings, Children's Centres, mainstream schools, academies, special schools and pupil referral units (PRUs), through to further education (FE) and sixth form colleges have numerous partnerships with external agencies, that is, anything from 50 to 150 different partnerships in a full service extended school.

Implementing effective multi-agency collaborative partnership working in any setting, as an aspect of the Every Child Matters Change for Children initiative, takes considerable time, and is not without its problems in removing cross-service barriers and redrawing boundaries. The practicalities of adopting a multi-agency approach can be problematic initially, as illustrated by this Sure Start project manager's comment:

> The availability of teaching staff is often different to the availability of social services staff, which is often different to the availability of health staff because of the demands that these professions have at different times of the day. It's about breaking down the behaviours that we have known for a long time. (Coleman, 2006: 27)

On a more optimistic note about multi-agency working, a behaviour support worker commented: 'The multi-agency approach means that we can look more holistically at the problem and talk as a team holistically about the problem ... ' (DfES, 2005: 55).

A director of a children's centre in Thanet also remarked: 'When you can hear a community worker, play worker and health visitor discussing plans for a child – no hours on the phone or reams of paperwork – you think, "Yes", this is the model of practice for the 21st century' (Sure Start, 2006: 13).

This book will enable busy practising, and aspiring, practitioners from education, health, social care, voluntary and community organizations to adopt a solution focused approach to multi-agency partnership working in order to:

- understand and value the different contributions each agency brings

- know how best to work collaboratively together

- know how to evaluate the impact of interventions and partnership working in relation to improving the Every Child Matters outcomes.

There are a number of detailed guidance documents and tool kits available on multi-agency partnership working, which can be downloaded from the government's Every Child Matters website (www.everychildmatters.gov.uk).

This book will appeal to practising and aspiring front-line children's workforce practitioners as it brings together in one concise volume a wealth of information and good practice, and presents this in a no nonsense, at-a-glance, user-friendly format, which makes sense of multi-agency partnership working in an educational setting.

What matters to every children's workforce practitioner is knowing, through telling evidence, that their collaborative support and interventions really do make a difference to the lives and well-being of children and young people. Enjoy using this practical resource to guide and inform your collaborative working practice, in securing better Every Child Matters outcomes.

How to use this book

The Every Child Matters change for children initiative is a huge agenda, and is still evolving, after it was first introduced by the government in its Green Paper *Every Child Matters* in September 2003. There is an overwhelming amount of information about Every Child Matters, with 600 documents available on the government's website. This book aims to demystify inter-professional working by helping all those practising and aspiring children's workforce practitioners involved in removing barriers to learning and improving children's well-being, to understand the principles, practice and expected outcomes from effective joined-up collaborative multi-agency partnership working, within a range of educational settings and children's centres.

The book considers the developments in multi-agency partnership working, providing a brief overview of the origin, concept and principles in Chapter 1. It looks at the benefits and challenges of multi-agency partnership working in an educational setting in Chapter 2. Chapter 3 focuses on the practicalities of operating and managing productive multi-agency working, and offers useful strategies for sustaining successful partnerships. Chapter 4 takes a closer look at the Team Around the Child aspect of Every Child Matters, and the implications for settings. The features of good practice in multi-agency partnership working is covered in Chapter 5. Chapter 6 provides advice and offers useful tools for evaluating the impact and outcomes of multi-agency provision and partnership working.

The format for each chapter is similar:

- The main points of the chapter are highlighted at the beginning.

- A checklist of practical tips for best practice is provided.

- Exemplar resources and materials for inter-professional development work are included.

- Signposting to further information, resources and websites are offered.

- Points to remember at the end of the chapter are provided as prompts.

- Further activities provide questions for reflection and future inter-professional multi-agency development work, which are appropriate for those who are trainee and practising children's workforce practitioners.

All chapters include photocopiable resources, which provide a useful starting point for inter-professional discussion and further development work. These resources can be customized and adapted to suit the context of the educational setting, where multi-agency practitioners are working in partnership.

I hope the book will give all those practising and aspiring children's workforce practitioners involved in improving children and young people's Every Child Matters well-being outcomes the confidence to understand the complexities of multi-agency partnership working, by enabling them to make informed choices about the best collaborative approaches to adopt in the particular educational setting they are working in.

Downloadable materials

Downloadable materials for this book can be found at www.sagepub.co.uk/cheminais for use in your setting. For a full list please see below.

Chapter 1

Figure 1.2   Checklist for developing effective multi-agency partnership working

Table 1.3   Joint inter-professional visioning and development activity

Table 1.4   Common core of skills and knowledge for multi-agency working

Table 1.6   Professional Standards for Teachers and multi-professional knowledge

Table 1.7   National Occupational Standards for Supporting Teaching and Learning in Schools – working with colleagues

Chapter 2

Figure 2.1   SWOT analysis for multi-agency partnership working

Figure 2.2   Force-field analysis framework for multi-agency partnership working

Figure 2.3   Diamond ranking template

Figure 2.4   Checklist for building the multi-agency team

Table 2.1   Benefits practitioners bring to multi-agency team-working

Table 2.2   Benefits of collaborative multi-agency partnership working

Table 2.3   Personal profile for multi-agency practitioners

Table 2.4   External service/agency information sheet

Chapter 3

Figure 3.1   Checklist for operating a multi-agency team in an educational setting

Figure 3.2   Checklist for managing change for multi-agency collaboration

Task 3.1   Changing practice

Task 3.2   What helps to effect change?

Key for icons

Chapter objectives

Further activities

Further information

Photocopiables

Tasks

1

The Origin, Concept and Principles of Multi-Agency Partnership Working

This chapter explains:

- Where multi-agency partnership working originated from
- The current terminology relating to multi-agency partnership working
- The key principles of effective multi-agency partnership working in educational settings and children's centres
- The skills and knowledge required by practitioners in the children's workforce for multi-agency working

This chapter is useful to those who work directly with children/young people.

The origin of multi-agency partnership working

Multi-agency partnership working is not a new development. As early as the mid-nineteenth century, health and social services were working together to endeavour to reduce poverty in England. It wasn't really until the 1980s, during the Thatcher government years, that the foundations of multi-agency partnership working were laid. The Children Act 1989 established the statutory requirement for inter-agency collaboration and joint working in relation to children and young people, requiring professionals to 'work together better'.

The 1990s saw the development of multilateral partnerships where public, private and voluntary sector organizations joined together to tackle cross-cutting issues, such as social exclusion, community safety and neighbourhood regeneration. Partnership overload and fatigue began to occur, resulting in the need for practitioners from multi-agencies to begin to reflect upon where and when the partnership 'bandwagon' should stop.

The last two decades have seen several government-funded initiatives aimed at promoting integrated services and more co-ordinated partnership working. For example, Sure Start, Children's Fund, Youth Offending Teams, BEST and Connexions, have all promoted multi-agency working.

Despite the introduction of government legislation and initiatives during this time to promote closer multi-agency partnership working, there existed:

- a lack of information sharing across agencies and services

- duplicated assessments to identify needs and subsequent provision

- poorly co-ordinated integrated activities across agencies

- too much 'buck passing' and referring on of clients between agencies

- a lack of continuity and inconsistent levels of service provision

- unclear accountability.

As part of *Every Child Matters* (DfES, 2003), the Children Act 2004 strengthened the requirement for agencies to work together more closely in multidisciplinary teams in order to improve the five Every Child Matters well-being outcomes for children and young people. This important piece of legislation responded to the Lord Laming inquiry into the tragic death of Victoria Climbié, which was the result of poor co-ordination and the failure of inter-agency communication in sharing information across agencies.

In relation to multi-agency partnership working, the Children Act 2004 required local authorities (LAs) partnership arrangements, via Children's Trusts to:

- identify the needs, circumstances and aspirations of children and young people

- agree the contribution each agency will make to meeting the Every Child Matters outcomes

- improve information sharing between agencies

- oversee arrangements for agencies to work collaboratively in the commissioning, delivery and integration of services.

In terms of schools' engagement with multi-agency partnership working, it was largely community schools, full service extended schools, and special schools that had well-established practice. In mainstream schools it was variable, according to the context and complexity of the needs of their pupil populations, for example, looked after children (LAC), special educational needs/learning difficulties and disabilities (SEN/LDD) and other vulnerable 'at risk' groups. The government's recent extended school and children's centre initiative which builds on this existing good practice, are considered to make a significant contribution in responding to the Every Child Matters agenda, by acting as service 'hubs' for the local community: 'An extended school is a school that recognises that it cannot work alone in helping children and young people to achieve their potential, and therefore decides to work in partnership with other agencies that have an interest in outcomes for children and young people, and with the local community' (Piper, 2005: 2).

The government acknowledged the value of multi-agency partnership working with extended schools to address children and young people's problems: 'Having key professionals such as health workers, psychologists and youth workers based on school sites and working closely alongside teachers means that children's problems can be addressed more effectively, with less disruption to their learning' (DfES, 2002: 4).

Extended schools and children's centres enable professional boundaries to be redrawn through the adoption of greater interdependence between teachers and multi-agency front-line workers, where mutual respect, trust and collaborative team effort become regular practice.

One extended school co-ordinator commented: 'Without ECM, there is little that the services would have in common. Everyone is singing from the same hymn sheet and ECM has broadened their outlook. If it wasn't for the agenda it would have been a real struggle' (Wilkin et al., 2008: 9).

Children's centres

Sure Start children's centres are multi-purpose centres that bring together childcare, early education, health, employment and support services for pre-school children and families. Children's centres aim to help children, and particularly disadvantaged children, to improve their life chances through better educational achievement and healthy living, and to support families and help parents to return to work or find better employment opportunities. Public, private and voluntary providers work together in a children's centre. The services they provide include:

- integrated early education and childcare, available 10 hours a day, five days a week, and 48 weeks a year

- baby weighing and health visitors

- health checks

- links to Jobcentre Plus

- crèche

- antenatal and post-natal services

- speech and language development

- training sessions

- support networks for childminders

- play sessions

- baby massage

- signposting to employment opportunities

- support for children and parents with special needs

- pre- and post-natal classes

- home visits to families

- play sessions in community settings

- mobile toy libraries.

Extended schools

Extended schools provide a range of services and activities beyond the school day, from 8 a.m. to 6 p.m., to help meet the needs of its pupils, their families and the wider community. The extended school core offer includes:

- **high-quality wrap-around childcare** available from 8 a.m. to 6 p.m. all year round

- **a varied menu of activities** which can include homework clubs, study support, sport, music tuition, dance and drama, arts and crafts, special interest clubs such as chess and first aid courses, volunteering, business and enterprise activities, visits to museums and galleries, and learning a foreign language

- **parenting support** which includes information sessions for parents at phase transfer, information about national and local sources of advice, guidance and further information, parenting programmes and family learning sessions

- **swift and easy referral** to a wide range of specialist support services such as speech therapy, Child and Adolescent Mental Health Services (CAMHS), family support services, intensive behaviour support, and (for young people) sexual health services. Some of these services may be delivered on or near the school site

- **providing wider community access** to information and communication technology (ICT), sports and arts facilities, including adult learning.

The concept of multi-agency partnership working

Multi-agency partnership working is where practitioners from more than one agency work together jointly, sharing aims, information, tasks and responsibilities in order to intervene early to prevent problems arising which may impact on children's learning and achievement. Multi-agency working involves the joint planning and delivery of co-ordinated services that are responsive to children and young people's changing needs. As one practitioner comments: '[Multi-agency] Inter-agency working is about making sure that people are regularly talking about their work, understanding each others' roles and sharing with other agencies and service users. It is about working together towards commonly agreed aims and objectives' (McInnes, 2007: 5).

There are a number of related terms and concepts that are used interchangeably in documentation, which reflect a range of structures, approaches and rationales to multi-agency partnership working. These are as follows:

- **Inter-agency working** is where more than one agency work together in a planned and formal way.

- **Integrated working** is where practitioners work together, adopting common processes to deliver front-line services, co-ordinated and built around the needs of children and young people.

- **Multi-professional/multidisciplinary working** is where staff with different professional backgrounds and training work together.

- **Joint working** is when professionals from more than one agency work together on a specific project or initiative.

- **Partnership working** refers to the processes that build relationships between different groups of professionals and services at different levels, to get things done. It entails two or more organizations or groups of practitioners joining together to achieve something they could not do alone, sharing a common problem or issue and collectively taking responsibility for resolving it. 'Partnership' therefore refers to a way of working as well as to a form of organization.

In relation to multi-agency working with educational settings to improve pupils' ECM outcomes, collaborative partnership working must add value to the efforts of the educational organization, as well as provide services outside the realm of school staff expertise. Teachers will begin to understand, recognize and accept that practitioners from other services can address pupils' well-being needs best, thus allowing them to focus on their core role of teaching and facilitating learning.

The five degrees of multi-agency partnership working

- **Coexistence** – clarity between practitioners from different agencies as to who does what and with whom.

- **Co-operation** – practitioners from different agencies sharing information and recognizing the mutual benefits and value of partnership working, that is, pooling the collective knowledge, skills and achievements available.

- **Co-ordination** – partners planning together; sharing some roles and responsibilities, resources and risk-taking; accepting the need to adjust and make some changes to improve services, thus avoiding overlap.

- **Collaboration** – longer-term commitments between partners, with organizational changes that bring shared leadership, control, resources and risk-taking. Partners from different agencies agree to work together on strategies or projects, each contributing to achieving shared goals.

- **Co-ownership** – practitioners from different agencies commit themselves to achieving a common vision, making significant changes in what they do and how they do it.

In particular, good co-ordination, co-operation and collaboration produce efficient multi-agency working, which adds value for educational settings, that is, it increases the organization's skills and capacity to improve and meet children and young people's Every Child Matters well-being needs.

The five stages of participation

David Wilcox (2000) produced a ladder of participation, which he had adapted from Sherry Arnstein's 1969 version, which had eight stages, and related to the involvement of citizens in planning processes in the USA. Wilcox's ladder comprises five stages. Stage one has the lowest degree of participation and control. Stages three to five have the highest degrees of participation and control, and are examples of substantial participation and true partnership working. Table 1.1a provides an overview of David Wilcox's ladder of participation, which has great relevance to multi-agency partnership working, and Table 1.1b is the partnership ladder offered by Gaster et al.

†††† Ladder of participation multi-agency task

Each member of the educational setting's multi-agency team is to answer the following questions individually, and then discuss their responses collectively, with other team members, in order to compare and contrast findings.

- Where are you on the ladder of participation in relation to your multi-agency partnership?

- How inclusive is the multi-agency partnership?

Table 1.1a   Ladder of participation

Stage on ladder	Features
5. Supporting	Helping others to do what they want within a supportive framework which may offer resources as well as advice
4. Acting together	The different interests together decide what is best, forming a partnership to carry it out
3. Deciding together	Encouraging team practitioners to provide additional ideas and options, and jointly decide which is the best way forward
2. Consultation	Identify problems, offering a number of options, solutions, and listening to the feedback from others
1. Information	Telling the team and other stakeholders what is planned

Source: Wilcox, 2000: 4–5

Table 1.1b   Gaster et al. ladder of multi-agency partnership working

Stage on ladder	Features
5. **Collaboration and full partnership**	Involving separate and distinct roles but shared values and agenda. Pooled resources blurred boundaries, continuously developing to meet changing needs. Less powerful partners are supported to play a full role
4. **Co-ordination and co-operation in practice**	Involving active co-ordination processes; co-ordinator knows what is going on, draws on each (autonomous) partner as appropriate, helps to nurture developmental and co-operative culture and involve and support new partners
3. **Implementing projects and service plans**	Joint or separately taken action on agreed plan, identify monitoring methods and review processes, mutual feedback on success/failure
2. **Planning action**	Involving identifying local and service needs where cross boundary working is needed and could be effective. Debate of local needs and priorities, agree different partners contributions, decide actions and processes. Identify (the need for) new partners
1. **Information exchange**	Involving mutual learning, knowledge of what each partner does and could do, openness about decision-making processes, new methods of access to information (including IT)

Source: Percy-Smith, 2005: 28–9

- How do you ensure practitioners from the voluntary sector joining the team feel valued as much as public sector practitioners?

- How is the multi-agency team you work in developing its partnership capacity?

Key drivers of multi-agency working

There are three main key drivers of multi-agency working in any educational set-ting, according to Andy Coleman (2006):

- **Promoting the interests of children and related legal imperatives** – for exam-ple, collaborating to meet the needs of children with disabilities, SEN, children in public care (LAC), vulnerable children whose welfare is at risk and who need safeguarding.

- **Promoting joined-up thinking and Every Child Matters** – which focuses on well-co-ordinated services meeting the needs of the whole child through responding to the five ECM well-being outcomes: being healthy, staying safe, enjoying and achieving, making a positive contribution, and achieving economic well-being.

- **Collaborative advantage** – requiring a range of skills and expertise existing among different practitioners to be brought together in order to add value and be more responsive to preventing children's problems arising, which create barriers to learning.

Parton and Vangen (2004: 2) comment: 'To gain real advantage from any collaboration, something has to be achieved that could not have been achieved by any one of the agencies acting alone.'

Coleman (2006: 9) refers to Tony Blair's speech of 1997 when he commented: 'Joined-up problems demand joined-up solutions.'

Models of multi-agency working

There is no blueprint for multi-agency working. The Department for Children, Schools and Families (DCSF) offers three different models for setting up multi-agency services to support educational settings, in improving ECM outcomes for children and young people. Table 1.2 describes the characteristics of the three models which are the multi-agency panel; the multi-agency team; and the integrated service.

Atkinson et al. offer five models of multi-agency activity. These are:

- **Decision-making groups**, which provide a forum in which professionals from different agencies meet and discuss issues and make decisions, largely at a strategic level.

- **Consultation and training**, whereby professionals from one agency enhance the expertise of those from another, usually at an operational level.

- **Centre-based delivery**, gathering a range of expertise on one site in order to deliver a more co-ordinated and comprehensive service. Services may not be delivered jointly, but exchange of information and ideas is facilitated.

- **Co-ordinated delivery**, whereby the appointment of a co-ordinator to pull together disparate services facilitates a more cohesive response to need through a collaboration between agencies involved in the delivery of services. Delivery by professionals is at an operational level, while the co-ordinator also operates strategically.

- **Operational team delivery**, in which professionals from different agencies work together on a day-to-day basis forming a cohesive multi-agency team delivering services directly to clients (Atkinson et al., 2002: 11–23).

Figure 1.1 illustrates the eight essential building blocks needed for effective multi-agency working.

Table 1.2　Characteristics of the three models of multi-agency working

Multi-agency model	Key characteristics
Multi-agency panel	• Panel is co-ordinated by a chair • Most meetings are arranged by the panel manager • There is usually a good mix of agencies represented • Practitioners remain employed by their home agency • The panel or network meets monthly or every term to discuss children with additional needs who would benefit from multi-agency input, and to review their work • Panel members may carry out case work themselves, or employ key workers to lead on case work • An example of this type of model is a Youth Inclusion and Support Panel, or Team Around the Child
Multi-agency team	• There is a dedicated team leader who works to a common purpose and common goals • There is a good mix of staff from different disciplines who are seconded or recruited into the team • There is a strong team identity • Practitioners may maintain links with their home agencies for supervision and training • There is scope to engage in work with universal services and at a range of levels – not just with individual children and young people, but also small group, family and whole-school work • An example of this type of model includes Behaviour and Education Support Teams (BEST), and Youth Offending Teams (YOTs)
Integrated service	• Acts as a service hub for the community, usually on one site • Usually delivered from school/early years settings • A range of separate services share a common location, vision and principles in working together • Commitment by partner providers to fund/facilitate integrated service delivery • Services usually include health, specialist advice and guidance, outreach and adult learning • Collective inter-professional training strategies are often present • Examples include children's centres and extended schools offering access to integrated, multi-agency services

Source: CWDC, 2007: 1–2

The key principles of multi-agency partnership working

Different agencies work at different speeds; for example, education works at a rapid pace, while health services take more time working with clients. Listed below are the key principles for effective multi-agency partnership working within any educational setting.

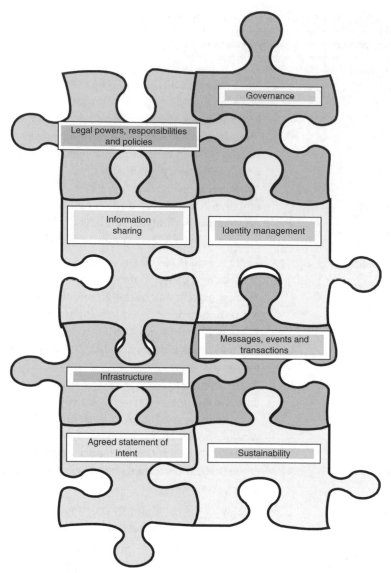

Figure 1.1   Framework for working in a multi-agency partnership: the eight essential building blocks of the framework for working in a multi-agency environment

- Adequate lead-in time has been provided to establish multi-agency partnership working within the educational setting.

- Existing good practice in multi-agency partnership within the setting has been built upon.

- There is an agreed, shared partnership principle based around the underlying aims and philosophy of Every Child Matters.

- A common professional language and terminology is utilized between different agencies and within the educational setting.

- Practitioners' respective roles and responsibilities are clear and understood.

- The contributions of all practitioners working directly with pupils to remove barriers to learning and improve their well-being are valued.

- Procedures and protocols for multi-agency referral, assessment, interventions and service provision are clear.

- Regular opportunities are provided for ongoing joint inter-professional training and development.

- A comprehensive induction programme exists for any new practitioners joining the educational setting.

- Regular meetings, at least once each half term, are held between key staff in the educational setting and the multi-agency practitioners to monitor, evaluate and review impact and outcomes of provision on targeted pupils.

- Multi-agency practitioners are able to contribute to the educational setting's improvement planning, self-evaluation and decision-making processes in order to inform future developments.

- Practitioners from multi-agencies are represented on the senior leadership team (SLT) and/or on the governing body or the management board of the educational setting.

- Pupils and their parents/carers receiving multi-agency support and interventions, have opportunities to review their own progress and comment on service provision.

- Pupil-level attainment and ECM well-being data is analysed and used to inform multi-agency provision.

- Protected time is guaranteed for multi-agency joint working.

†††† Inter-professional development tasks

Invite a group of representative key staff from the educational setting as well as practitioners from the multi-agencies/VCS organizations that are working directly with pupils in the setting, to get together to form a working group. Undertake the two developmental tasks together, in the mixed working group. Bring together the findings from the two activities, to form an overall agreed joint statement of purpose, common goals, a mission statement and a partnership agreement.

Task 1.1: Agreeing a common purpose and goals

1. On flip-chart paper draw a large circle in the centre, and then draw an outer circle.

2. Ask each member of the group to write down on Post-it notes **three** statements about what they think the multi-agency team's main purpose and goals should be.

3. Participants place their statements in the inner circle on the flip chart.

4. The whole group reads through all the statements and moves any it considers not to be relevant or important to the outer circle.

5. The facilitator of the task asks the group to consider the remaining statements in the inner circle.

6. The working group writes down the agreed main purpose and the agreed goals for the multi-agency partnership, working within the educational setting or children's centre.

For Task 1.2 use Table 1.3.

The skills and knowledge required for multi-agency working

Members of the wider children's workforce include: police officers, doctors, nurses, teachers, teaching assistants, learning mentors, nursery staff, social workers, therapists, youth workers, leisure and recreational workers, housing staff and those practitioners who work in criminal/youth justice, mental health or drug and alcohol services. All these practitioners work together to provide services that fully meet the needs of children, young people and their parents or carers.

All these practitioners (colleagues) from public, private and voluntary sector services have to meet the common core of skills and knowledge required for effective multi-agency working, which is one of six areas of expertise.

Table 1.4 provides an overview of what the common core of skills and knowledge for multi-agency working are.

The joint statement on inter-professional work with colleagues

The General Social Care Council (GSCC), the General Teaching Council for England (GTC) and the Nursing and Midwifery Council (NMC) produced a joint statement in summer 2007, which sets out the values and dispositions underpinning effective inter-professional work with children and young people. The joint statement can be viewed at www.nmc-uk.org/interprof.

Table 1.5 shows the inter-professional values of the joint statement.

Professional Standards for Teachers

The Training and Development Agency for Schools (TDA) in September 2007 indicated that the Professional Standards for Teachers are underpinned by the five Every Child Matters outcomes as well as the six areas of the common core of skills and knowledge for the children's workforce. Table 1.6 provides an overview of the relevant Qualified Teacher Status (QTS) and the core professional standards for all teachers, which relate to multi-professional/inter-professional working.

Table 1.3 Joint inter-professional visioning and development activity

Multi-agency aspect	Education perspective	Health perspective	Social Care perspective	VCS/Other e.g. police, YOT, perspective	Overall joint inter-professional agreed statement
In this educational setting multi-agency partnership working means …					
The mission statement for multi-agency partnership working in this educational setting should be …					
Together, in partnership with the educational setting, multi-agency practitioners will improve the Every Child Matters outcomes for children and young people by …					
In order to ensure multi-agency partnership working is effective in this educational setting and meets the agreed aims, I/we will need to …					
The barriers that may prevent effective multi-agency partnership working taking place are …					
These barriers can be overcome by …					
By the end of one year I/we hope to have achieved through collaborative multi-agency partnership working, the following …					

Photocopiable:

Effective Multi-Agency Partnerships, Sage Publications © Rita Cheminais, 2009

□   A joint visioning and awareness raising event/workshop has taken place on ECM and collaborative partnership working in the educational setting.

□   The aims, goals, principles and purpose of partnership working are clear.

□   It is clear what all practitioners/partners bring to the joint activity and team.

□   Realistic expectations exist as to what the partnership can hope to achieve.

□   Careful consideration has been given to practitioners' diversity, culture, sensitivities and professional background.

□   Realistic agreed targets, objectives and milestones have been set.

□   Respective roles and responsibilities of members of the joint partnership are clear.

□   Partnership working is based on shared values, trust and mutual respect.

□   Good, open two-way communication exists between practitioners.

□   Appropriate accommodation and ICT within the educational setting for multi-agency service delivery facilitate information sharing.

□   Opportunities exist for joint inter-professional team building and solution-focused problem solving.

□   Line management and accountability procedures are clear for multi-agency practitioners working in the educational setting.

□   Clear procedures exist for the joint monitoring and evaluation of outcomes.

□   Sufficient quality time is provided to staff within the educational setting as well as to multi-agency practitioners to enable them to meet jointly together to review progress and plan future improvements and developments.

□   Key review and developmental multi-agency meetings have been scheduled in advance for the next 12 months.

Figure 1.2   Checklist for developing effective multi-agency partnership working

Table 1.4   Common core of skills and knowledge for multi-agency working

Skills	**Knowledge**
Communication and teamwork	**Your role and remit**
• Communicate effectively with other practitioners and professionals by listening and ensuring that you are being listened to	• Know your main job and responsibilities within your working environment
• Appreciate that others may not have the same understanding of professional terms and may interpret abbreviations such as acronyms differently	• Know the value and expertise you bring to a team and that brought by your colleagues
	Know how to make queries
• Provide timely, appropriate, succinct information to enable other practitioners to deliver their support to young	• Know your role within different group situations and how you contribute to the overall group process, understanding the value of sharing how you approach your role with other professionals
	• Develop your skills and knowledge with training from experts, to minimize the need for referral to specialist services, enabling

Table 1.4 (Continued)

Skills	Knowledge
person, the child or parent or carer	continuity for the family, child or young person while enhancing your own skills and knowledge
• Record, summarize, share and feed back information, using IT skills where necessary to do so	• Have general knowledge and understanding of the range of organisations and individuals working with children, young people and those caring for them, and be aware of the roles and responsibilities of other professionals
• Work in a team context, forging and sustaining relationships across agencies and respecting the contribution of others working with children, young people and families	
• Share experience through formal and informal exchanges and work with adults who are parents/carers	
Assertiveness	**Procedures and working methods**
• Be proactive, initiate necessary action and be able and prepared to put forward your own judgements	• Know what to do in given cases, e.g. for referrals or raising concerns
• Have the confidence to challenge situations by looking beyond your immediate role and asking considered questions	• Know what the triggers are for reporting incidents or unexpected behaviour
	• Know how to work within your own and other organizational values, beliefs and cultures
• Present facts and judgements objectively	• Know what to do when there is an insufficient response from other organizations or agencies, while maintaining a focus on what is in the child or young person's best interests
• Identify possible sources of support within your own working environment	
• Judge when you should provide the support yourself and when you should refer the situation to another practitioner or professional	• Understand the way that partner services operate – their procedures, objectives, role and relationships – in order to be able to work effectively alongside them
	• Know about the Common Assessment Framework for Children and Young People (CAF) and, where appropriate, how to use it
	The law, policies and procedures
	• Know about the existence of key laws relating to children and young people and where to obtain further information
	• Know about employers' safeguarding and health and safety policies and procedures, and how they apply in the wider working environment

Source: Her Majesty's Government, 2005: 18–20

Table 1.5   Joint statement of inter-professional values

Inter-professional work with colleagues

- Children's practitioners value the contribution that a range of colleagues make to children's lives, and they form effective relationships across the children's workforce. Their inter-professional practice is based on a willingness to bring their own expertise to bear on the pursuit of shared goals for children, and a respect for the expertise of others. Practitioners recognize that children and families, and colleagues, value transparency and reliability, and strive to make sure that processes, roles, goals and resources are clear
- Practitioners involved in inter-professional work recognize the need to be clear about lines of communication, management and accountability as these may be more complex than in their specialist setting
- They uphold the standards and values of their own professionals in their inter-professional work. They understand that sharing responsibility for children's outcomes does not mean acting beyond their competence or responsibilities
- They are committed to taking action if safety or standards are compromised, whether that means alerting their own manager/employer or another appropriate authority
- Children's practitioners understand that the knowledge, understanding and skills for inter-professional work may differ from those in their own specialism and they are committed to professional learning in this area as well as in their own field, through training and engagement with research and other evidence
- They are committed to reflecting on and improving their inter-professional practice, and to applying their inter-professional learning to their specialist work with children
- Work with children can be emotionally demanding, and children's practitioners are sensitive to and supportive of each other's well-being

Source: Nursing Midwifery Council (www.nmc-uk.org), General Social Care Council and the General Teaching Council for England, 2007

Table 1.6   Professional Standards for Teachers and multi-professional working

Qualified Teacher Status (QTS)	All teachers – core
Professional attributes	**Professional attributes**
Communicating and working with others	**Communicating and working with others**
Q4. Communicate effectively with children, young people, colleagues, parents and carers	C4(a) Communicate effectively with children, young people and colleagues
Q5. Recognize and respect the contribution that colleagues, parents and carers can make to the development and well-being of children and young people, and to raising the levels of attainment	C5. Recognize and respect the contributions that colleagues, parents and carers can make to the development and well-being of children and young people, and to raising their levels of attainment
Q6. Have a commitment to collaboration and co-operative working	C6. Have a commitment to collaboration and co-operative working where appropriate
Professional knowledge and understanding	**Professional knowledge and understanding**
Achievement and diversity	**Achievement and diversity**
Q20. Know and understand the roles of colleagues with specific responsibilities, including those with responsibility for learners with special educational needs	C20. Understand the roles of colleagues such as those having specific responsibilities for learners with special educational needs, disabilities and other individual

Table 1.6   (Continued)

Qualified Teacher Status (QTS)	All teachers – core
and disabilities and other individual learning needs	learning needs, and the contributions they can make to the learning, development and well-being of children and young people
Health and well-being Q21(b) Know how to identify and support children and young people whose progress, development or well-being is affected by changes or difficulties in their personal circumstances, and when to refer them to colleagues for specialist support	C21. Know when to draw on the expertise of colleagues, such as those with responsibility for the safeguarding of children and young people and special educational needs and disabilities, and to refer to sources of information, advice and support from external agencies
Professional skills **Team-working and collaboration** Q32. Work as a team member and identify opportunities for working with colleagues, sharing the development of effective practice with them Q33. Ensure that colleagues working with them are appropriately involved in supporting learning and understand the roles they are expected to fulfil	**Health and well-being** C25. Know how to identify and support children and young people whose progress, development or well-being is affected by changes or difficulties in their personal circumstances, and when to refer them to colleagues for specialist support
	Professional skills **Team-working and collaboration** C40. Work as a team member and identify opportunities for working with colleagues, managing their work where appropriate and sharing the development of effective practice with them C41. Ensure that colleagues working with them are appropriately involved in supporting learning and understand the roles they are expected to fulfil

Source: TDA, 2007b

The term 'colleagues' used in the professional standards refers to all those professionals with whom a teacher might work, that is, other teaching colleagues and the wider workforce within the educational setting, as well as other practitioners from external agencies working in the children's workforce.

The National Occupational Standards for supporting teaching and learning in schools

In June 2007 the TDA published the National Occupational Standards for supporting teaching and learning in schools, which were relevant to teaching assistants and other members of the school's children's workforce, other than teachers. These provide statements of competence relating to the skills and knowledge required to support teaching and learning in schools and other educational settings. They cover working with colleagues, as one of the five key areas of responsibility. These are outlined in Table 1.7

Table 1.7   National Occupational Standards for Supporting Teaching and Learning in Schools – working with colleagues

Unit number	Unit description
STL4	**Contribute to positive relationships** – with children, young people and adults, valuing people equally
STL5	**Provide effective support for your colleagues** – contributing to effective teamwork and maintaining working relationships with colleagues
STL20	**Develop and promote positive relationships** – communicate with adults, children and young people
STL21	**Support the development and effectiveness of work teams** – by being an effective member of a work team contributing to effective team practice
STL60	**Liaise with parents, carers and families** – facilitating information sharing while ensuring professional integrity in communications with parents, carers and families
STL62	**Develop and maintain working relationships with other practitioners** – doing what you can to support other practitioners work, utilizing your strengths and expertise in partnership working
STL63	**Provide leadership for your team** – provide direction to team members, and motivate and support them to achieve the teams and their own personal objectives. Allocate and check work in the team
STL64	**Provide leadership in your area of responsibility** – providing direction to colleagues in a specific programme, initiative or policy, motivating and supporting them to achieve the vision and objectives for the area
STL65	**Allocate and check work in your team** – fair and effective allocation of work to team members, checking on progress and quality of the team's work
STL66	**Lead and motivate volunteers** – briefing volunteers on their responsibilities and requirements, helping them to resolve any problems during volunteering activities, giving them feedback on their work and respecting their needs and preferences
STL67	**Provide learning opportunities for colleagues** – support colleagues in identifying their learning needs and provide opportunities to address these needs. Encourage colleagues to take responsibility for their own learning wherever possible
STL68	**Support learners by mentoring in the workplace** – plan the mentoring process, set up and maintain the mentoring relationship and provide mentoring to colleagues and trainees in the workplace
STL69	**Support competence achieved in the workplace** – assess staff performance in the workplace against agreed standards, and give them feedback on their performance

Source: TDA, 2007a

Table 1.8 Roles of some key multi-agency practitioners in schools

Police	Social care worker	School nurse	Housing officer
• Help to reduce truancy and exclusions	• Rapid response case work	• Provide confidential advice and guidance on a range of health-related issues including nutrition, exercise, smoking, mental health, drug abuse, sexual health	• Help to reduce antisocial behaviour among young people in the community by contributing to providing youth activities
• Reduce victimization, criminality and antisocial behaviour within the school and its community	• Parent/carers and family support, e.g. parent drop-ins, family learning classes		
• Help to identify and work with children/young people at risk of becoming victims of crime and bullying, or offenders	• Supporting transition from nursery to primary and from primary to secondary school	• Promote good health and support children and young people to make healthy life choices	• Provide funding, buildings and land for youth, community and environmental projects
• Support school staff in dealing with incidents of crime, victimization or antisocial behaviour	• Anger management	• Contribute to the school's PSHE programme and the Healthy Schools initiative	• Help to build greater understanding and positive relationships between the old and the young in the community through joint local history projects
• Promote the full participation of children/young people in the life of the school and its wider community	• Supporting the CAF process		
	• Supporting the school's PSHE programme	• Help to develop and update the school's health and safety policy and the sex education policy	
• Provide educational inputs for pupils in the classroom on aspects of citizenship and personal safety as part of PSHE, e.g. covering topics such as drugs, alcohol and bullying	• Signposting to specialist services		
	• Counselling and mentoring	• Provide advice on healthy school meals, and access to drinking water for pupils	• Work in close collaboration with other services, e.g. police, youth service
	• Relationship-building between schools and families		
• Work in partnership with other agencies such as the Youth Offending Team (YOT), Youth Justice, and Connexions	• Group and one-to-one support for children and young people	• Contribute to the school's extended services provision by running an after school	
	• Pupil support for bereavement, self-esteem, behaviour and attendance, depression, self-harming, school anxiety/phobia, family violence, substance abuse, bullying, suicidal threats		
	• Act as an advocate for children, young people and their families		

Table 1.8 (Continued)

Police	Social care worker	School nurse	Housing officer
• Build positive relationships between the police and young people	• Deliver workshops and seminars to teachers and other school staff, related to social-emotional and risk issues such as: how to manage pupils' behaviour in the classroom • Help to identify school staff and other agency practitioners who can help to maximize pupil success	healthy eating cookery club • Provide a drop-in clinic for children, young people and their parents on, or near, the school site • Support individual pupils with long term medical needs health plans • Support the safeguarding work of the school by advising staff • Provide immunisation to pupils, where appropriate • Run parent groups	to inform provision for young people in the community • Consult with children and young people on the facilities and services they want in the local community • Provide inputs to the school curriculum on housing education and homelessness • Help school staff to prepare pupils for leaving home and finding a home of their own • Provide information and advice to young people on housing choices, housing benefits, getting a mortgage, how to choose the right property • Advise school staff on how to support the learning of pupils who are in temporary accommodation

Points to remember

- Everyone brings skills, knowledge and expertise to multi-agency partnership working, which should be valued, respected and acknowledged.
- Do not reinvent the wheel, but build on existing good multi-agency partnership working practice.
- Ensure service users (pupils, parents/carers) have a 'voice and choice' in multi-agency provision.
- Every Child Matters provides the 'gel' and moral purpose that holds multi-agency collaborative partnership working together within the educational setting or children's centre.

Further activities

The following questions, based on aspects covered in this chapter, are designed to enable staff from within the educational setting or children's centre, in partnership with front-line practitioners from multi-agencies working directly with pupils, to discuss and identify ways forward in establishing agreed collaborative partnership working principles and practice.

- What do practitioners understand the term 'shared culture' to mean?

- What is the agreed vision, direction and approach on which multi-agency partnership working in the educational setting is based?

- What principles of inter-professional working have you jointly agreed upon to ensure effective multi-agency partnership working occurs?

- How have you ensured that the vision, aims and principles, jointly developed for multi-agency partnership working meet and match the identified needs of pupils with additional needs?

- How do you intend collectively to make the aims, purpose and principles of joint multi-professional/inter-professional partnership working explicit to a range of stakeholders in the educational setting or children's centre, and within the local community?

- What joint marketing campaign will you develop to help raise awareness among the teaching staff, teaching assistants (TAs), governors, pupils, parents/carers and local community members about the rationale, purpose and role of the multi-agency team working with pupils in the educational setting?

- What are the key ingredients' identified by stakeholders, of effective multi-agency partnership working and provision within the educational setting or children's centre, and what does it look like?

- What are the expectations of what multi-agency partnerships should achieve within the educational setting or children's centre?

Further information

The following websites have downloadable resources that support the aspects covered in this chapter.

www.partnerships.org.uk   This website has a good range of resources linked to partnerships, which has been put together by David Wilcox.

www.cwdcouncil.org.uk   This website provides a useful fact sheet on multi-agency working.

www.ecm.gov.uk/multiagencyworking   This website contains a great deal of information about establishing multi-agency working, and offers a tool kit for managers and practitioners. The web-based resource 'Getting started in multi-agency working' covers the following aspects: the benefits, challenges and success factors of multi-agency working; practical advice for setting up services; case study examples, and a common language glossary for practitioners.

http://lmscontent.ncsl.org.uk/ECM/   This website provides a range of useful documents and resources about ECM and multi-agency partnership working from a school leadership perspective.

Do not forget to also visit the Sage website (www.sagepub.co.uk/cheminais) for downloadable resources to use with this chapter.

2

The Benefits and Challenges of Collaborative Multi-Agency Working

> **This chapter describes:**
>
> - The latest research findings on how schools are implementing ECM and engaging collaboratively with other services and agencies
> - The benefits of multi-agency partnership working within educational settings
> - The challenges faced by educational settings in establishing and developing multi-agency partnership working
> - Positive ways forward in meeting the challenges and building the multi-agency team

This chapter is suitable for those who are researching multi-agency working.

Recent research into Every Child Matters and multi-agency working

Engagement in Every Child Matters is necessary because the intrinsic links between the educational setting, services, agencies and the community help to improve the educational achievement, the health and the social choices of children, young people and their families. The government continues to encourage schools and other educational settings to collaborate with each other and with outside agencies and organizations, in order to deliver the five ECM outcomes.

One local authority strategic manager commented in a recent National Foundation for Educational Research (NFER) report on the value of social care professionals working in extended schools: 'ECM has been the tool that people can identify with and say, well, although I sit in health or social care, or extended schools, I have a part to play ... and it is actually coming from the Government' (Wilkin et al., 2008: 9).

There have been a number of research studies and surveys on the implementation of the Every Child Matters agenda in schools, and how they are responding to the need for greater partnership working with other services and agencies.

The National Foundation for Educational Research in two annual surveys of trends in education 2006 and 2007, reported on how the Every Child Matters agenda was affecting schools. Both surveys identified the following main changes occurring as a result of schools engaging with Every Child Matters:

- school improvement planning reflecting the five ECM outcomes

- review of the curriculum and current school practice

- review of staffing and recruitment in school to align ECM with workforce remodelling

- marked growth in partnership involvement and information sharing

- increased extended school work

- improved school meals and greater awareness of healthy eating and healthy lifestyles

The two NFER surveys on ECM also identified the same challenges facing schools, in delivering the Every Child Matters agenda. These were:

- financial issues, particularly in relation to sustainability of resources

- having sufficient time to develop and implement the ECM agenda

- developing closer collaboration with other services and agencies involved in supporting children and young people's well-being.

The NFER surveys of 2006 and 2007 both found that schools had more contact with some local services than others. For example, 90 per cent of primary and secondary schools surveyed accessed health, social care and the police more than housing services, which were accessed by only 41 per cent of primary schools and 50 per cent of secondary schools. Housing and social care were the two services which were considered to be the least accessible for support by schools.

The General Teaching Council published a report in autumn 2007 on Every Child Matters and the Children's Workforce in schools (GTC, 2007a). In relation to collaborative working between schools and multi-agency front-line practitioners the report highlighted the need for the following:

- sufficient well-trained, high-quality front-line practitioners from services and agencies with the capacity to respond effectively to the ECM agenda in order to deliver preventative interventions

- greater opportunities for more inter-professional learning, training and development between school staff and multi-agency practitioners working directly with pupils in the school to improve integrated working

- inter-professional training in using inter-agency frameworks and protocols, that is, National Service Framework, (NSF), the Common Assessment Framework, ContactPoint

- the time to invest in building quality relationships between school staff and multi-agency front-line practitioners

- clearer and improved information for schools on where to refer children to and who to seek specific expertise from

- more up-to-date information about voluntary sector provision available

- more information and a clearer understanding about the expertise, role, procedures and processes of children's services and agencies working with schools

- opportunities to get together and work with colleagues from other services to develop an analysis of local needs which can be addressed collaboratively

- greater sharing of exemplification of good practice in how to implement ECM and multi-agency partnership working in educational settings

- more support for educational settings in relation to accountability for monitoring and evaluating the impact of multi-agency interventions and support on improving pupils ECM well-being outcomes.

Harris, A. et al., reported on *Understanding the reasons why schools do or do not fully engage with the ECM/ES agenda*, on behalf of the NCSL and the TDA.

Their report findings confirmed those of the NFER and the GTC, in the need for:

- greater clarity of purpose in connection with other agencies

- schools establishing and consolidating links with partners and other agencies

- schools creating a shared vision, purpose and goals with other agencies

- a common understanding of the professional language used across different multi-professional disciplines

- schools establishing a clear line of communication, accountability and decision making with other agencies

- greater involvement of outside agencies on the school's leadership team

- whole-school staff training on strategies for fostering multi-agency ways of working together

- shared evaluative feedback existing between schools and multi-agencies

- a clear understanding of the respective roles and responsibilities of partners and agencies in the implementation of ECM

- sufficient local authority support to facilitate and secure multi-agency inputs for schools, including ring-fenced funding to develop and cement such partnership working

- designated staff in schools to have the time to co-ordinate the wide-ranging multi-agency partnerships for delivering ECM

- school leaders to focus more on interrelationship building, collaborative working, multi-agency leadership, in becoming more politically astute, in order to re-engineer and transform cultural, professional and organizational boundaries and practices.

The benefits of collaborative multi-agency working

There are many benefits of multi-agency collaborative partnership working for educational settings. Every Child Matters is the 'gel' that holds partnership working together, and the value it adds contributes immensely to improving the learning and well-being outcomes of children and young people.

The main benefits of collaborative multi-agency working, evident in everyday practice within a range of educational settings, are as follows:

- leads to enhanced and improved outcomes for children and young people, through a range of joined-up services, advice and support being readily available and easily accessible

- benefits teachers understanding of multi-agency practitioners' activities, and knowing about the services to signpost pupils to, enabling them to focus on their core role of teaching

- helps to build consensus, strengthen partnership voice, break down professional boundaries and parochial attitudes

- helps to enhance scale of coverage and sustainability when pooled budgets, joint bids, joint projects and endeavours are put into action

- can help to build a more cohesive community approach through united multi-agency practitioners taking greater ownership and responsibility for addressing local needs jointly, thus avoiding duplication or overlap of provision

- promotes mutual support, encouragement and the exchange of ideas between staff, helping the sharing of expertise, knowledge and resources for training and good practice, leading to more manageable workloads

- increased fit between the services offered and those required by children, young people and their families to meet their needs

- improved co-ordination of services resulting in better relationships, improved referrals and the addressing of joint targets

- offers a broader perspective or focus to working practice

- helps to improve understanding and raise awareness of issues and agencies, and other professionals practice

- increased level of trust existing between partners/providers in relation to everyone knowing each can and will deliver

- facilitates joint planning for future multi-agency developments

- increased staff morale knowing that they do not work in isolation and that issues and problems can be resolved collaboratively

- more enthusiastic and committed staff who have high expectations of them-selves and others.

An extended school co-ordinator in a secondary school commented: 'We benefit from having the experience of working with people from other backgrounds. We pick up other perspectives and others' ways of doing things' (Coleman, 2006: 14).

The challenges of collaborative multi-agency working

The challenges that are identified with multi-agency working arise largely as a result of the complexities involved when practitioners engage in collaborative ventures. The following main challenges are reflected in recent research into multi-agency working in schools and children's centres.

- Funding concerns in relation to sustainability, for example, conflicts over funding within and between different agencies; a general lack of funding for multi-agency training and development work and to cover accommodation and on-costs for service delivery.

- Time – only a finite amount of time available to respond to many different priorities; some services have waiting lists, for example, CAMHS

- Communication – ensuring clear routes for two-way communication between the educational setting, agencies and practitioners in order to exchange infor-mation and improve joined-up co-ordinated working.

- The danger of a lack of clarity arising about the roles and responsibilities of practitioners in a wider and more diverse children's workforce.

- Adapting to working in a new and different context, for example, a school or children's centre, as opposed to a hospital environment.

- Competing priorities placing multiple demands and expectations on educational settings and services, for example, Healthy Schools initiative, ECM, Building Schools for the Future (BSF), personalised learning, 14–19 agenda. Danger of initiative overload occurring if not well managed.

- The management of different professional and multi-agency service cultures, for example, staff recruitment and retention, disparities in status, pay, conditions of service, working hours and working conditions. Health works 24 hours a day, seven days a week and education does not.

- Understanding each other's professional language and protocols.

- Territorial issues – overcoming the reluctance to share equipment and facilities, professional jealousy and inter-agency mistrust.

- Preventing too much 'referring on' or 'passing the buck' becoming too regular an approach being adopted to give the illusion of effective action having been taken.

- Finding mutually convenient times for managers and practitioners to meet.

- Problems of cross-authority working where health authority (primary care trust – PCT) and the local authority boundaries are different.

- Additional stress and pressures arising from unsuccessful or disappointing attempts at multi-agency working having an adverse affect on staff morale and turnover.

- The assumption that multi-agency partnership working must be adopted at all times, even when it may be inappropriate in some instances.

- Lack of coherence in the aims, intentions and joined-up thinking between different agencies, resulting in role overlap or duplication of services.

- Staff resistance to change both within the educational setting and among multi-agency practitioners. A lack of understanding and appreciation about the reasons for change, and what the change process entails and the benefits it can bring to improving the ECM outcomes for children, young people and their families.

- Engaging the 'hard to reach' parents/carers, families, children and young people with multi-agency service provision, education and lifelong learning.

Positive ways forward in meeting the challenges

Schools and other educational settings are already contributing in a number of ways to improving the wider well-being of children and young people, however, they cannot do this alone. Every Child Matters provides a climate that fosters and encourages partnership working with external agency practitioners, who also recognize the school or other educational setting as being a valuable resource to help them fulfil their remit in relation to this huge agenda.

One extended school (ES) co-ordinator commented: 'We can't work in isolation from the ECM agenda because anything we do fits in with one category or another' (Kendall et al., 2007: 11).

Figure 2.1 and Figure 2.2 will help staff from within the educational setting, in partnership with front-line practitioners from multi-agencies, to examine their beliefs, strengths, and areas for development in meeting the challenges that Every Child Matters poses for them.

Choosing **one** of the following four ECM recommendations, complete the strengths, weaknesses, opportunities and threats (SWOT) analysis using Figure 2.1.

- To improve information sharing between agencies.

- To encourage the development of multi-agency services around schools and children's centres.

Figure 2.1   SWOT analysis for multi-agency partnership working

SWOT ANALYSIS	
Aspect of multi-agency partnership working to be addressed:	
STRENGTHS	**WEAKNESSES**
OPPORTUNITIES	**THREATS**

Figure 2.2 Force-field analysis framework for multi-agency partnership working

FORCE-FIELD ANALYSIS

The change required for enhancing multi-agency collaborative partnership working:

FORCES SUPPORTING CHANGE	FORCES PREVENTING CHANGE

STRATEGIES FOR SUSTAINABLE IMPLEMENTATION OF EFFECTIVE MULTI-AGENCY PARTNERSHIP WORKING

 Photocopiable:
Effective Multi-Agency Partnerships, Sage Publications © Rita Cheminais, 2009

- To improve the skills and effectiveness of those working in the children's workforce.

- To enable LAs to improve outcomes for children by commissioning services from the public, private and the voluntary sectors.

After undertaking this audit and awareness-raising exercise collaboratively, complete the next three activities using Table 2.1, Table 2.2 and Table 2.3

Harris, A. et al., (2007) identified four important developmental stages essential for building the capacity for the implementation of ECM/ES, and for sustainable multi-agency partnership working. These are:

1. Creating the internal conditions and structural infrastructure within the educational setting to support ECM/ES and multi-agency partnerships.This entails workforce remodelling, ECM/ES as a key priority on the development plan; promoting an inclusive 'can do' ethos and culture; shared moral purpose and focused distributed leadership; staff involvement in decision-making; targeted staff inter-professional development; positive staff collaboration; developing a learning culture of reflection and enquiry among practitioners, and aligning ECM/ES work activities more closely.

2. Developing clarity of purpose in the connection with other agencies. This involves establishing and consolidating links with partners and other agencies; creating a shared vision and purpose between partners; shared goals, evaluative feedback, establishing clear lines of communication and decision-making, and becoming a broker of multi-agency work.

3. Enhancing and extending community support and involvement. This entails setting up parents' groups; involving support workers, and establishing co-located services and the opportunities to work with other agencies.

4. Securing additional external support and additional funding in order to extend and sustain ECM/ES activities. This has involved the effective management of the internal and external conditions for change to support ECM/ES, through securing LA guidance, support, training and resourcing, local businesses and community support, as well as constantly seeking sponsorship and different sources of additional ring-fenced funding and resources to maintain extended school service provision (Harris et al., 2007: 8–9, 30).

Schools and children's centres where ECM/ES and multi-agency partnership working are successfully operating, have achieved this by adopting the four developmental stages. However, there have been other specific key factors that have successfully supported moving forward in relation to multi-agency partnership working:

- The concept of the community and the educational setting are intrinsically linked to improving the educational, health and social chances of children,

Figure 2.3 Diamond Ranking Template

Table 2.1   Benefits practitioners bring to multi-agency team-working

List all the benefits you will bring to the multi-agency team in the educational setting, over the indicated periods of time, and the expected measures of success.

Name: ———————————————— Service: ————————————————

Date: ————————————————

In the next month	In six months' time	In a year's time
Measures of success	**Measures of success**	**Measures of success**

Table 2.2 Benefits of collaborative multi-agency partnership working

Nine diamonds inter-professional multi-agency activity:

1. Read the 12 statements about the benefits of multi-agency partnership working in the box below, and discuss each one within your group.

2. Agree on three statements to discard.

3. Using the nine diamond template (Figure 2.3), put the remaining nine statements in order of priority, starting with the top diamond and working down to the last diamond.

4. Reach a consensus, about which are the **six** most important benefits of multi-agency partnership working, within the educational setting.

STATEMENTS

A. Taking part in joint activities and projects

B. Views being listened to by others

C. Able to effect change

D. Knowing contributions are valued

E. Sharing decision-making

F. Finding solutions to problems in partnership with others

G. Being respected by other practitioners

H. Sharing ideas, knowledge and expertise with other practitioners

I. Participating in regular inter-professional training

J. Understanding different practitioners' roles and responsibilities

K. Having an agreed vision, aims and objectives

L. Helping to remove children and young people's barriers to learning

---

Photocopiable:
Effective Multi-Agency Partnerships, Sage Publications © Rita Cheminais, 2009

Table 2.3 Personal profile for multi-agency practitioners

Your name: _____

Job title: _____

Contact details: _____

Briefly outline your role:

-
-
-
-
-
-

What have been your main successes and achievements in working with children in the educational setting?

-
-
-
-

What has been the most significant contribution you have made to multi-agency partnership working in the educational setting?

What **three** things would help to improve your work with children and young people in the educational setting?

1.

2.

3.

What aspects of multi-agency partnership working do you wish to improve or know more about, and receive inter-professional training on?

 Photocopiable:

Effective Multi-Agency Partnerships, Sage Publications © Rita Cheminais, 2009

young people and their families, and these stakeholders are actively engaged in identifying and informing services to meet local needs.

- The creation of five change teams that work on each of the five ECM outcomes, or on each of the five extended school core offer areas, that is, wrap-around childcare, a varied menu of activities, parenting support, swift and easy referral to a range of specialist support services, and providing wider community access to ICT, sports and arts facilities, including adult learning. These change teams include representatives from local stakeholders, for example, parents, children and young people, governors, school staff and practitioners from external agencies.

- Proactive parental and community representatives and pre-existing networks, for example, community development group, visible school head in the community, parent ambassadors, family liaison support workers all aiming to make a difference in the locality overall.

- School staff and multi-agency practitioners better informed about the requirements and opportunities that ECM/ES bring.

- Positive, optimistic and innovative leadership which has a vision of the possible; a belief in the whole child, parent and community centred approach to lifelong learning; willing to take risks; taking the wider outward looking community view, and understanding the local political context.

- Promoting relationship building and a team approach through distributed leadership and effective delegation to facilitate the more effective partnership working, which is supported by appropriate training and ongoing professional development.

- ECM and ES are integral to the learning process and pupil entitlement, viewed as central to everything that the educational setting does, and not perceived as a 'bolt-on' extra.

- Finding 'win-win' situations, where it is clear how the educational setting can enable multi-agencies to achieve their aims and, more importantly, to enable the educational setting in partnership with multi-agency practitioners to help each other to achieve the ECM aims.

- Providing sufficient quality protected 'time out' for practitioners from the different agencies, and key staff in the educational setting to meet up, get to know each other, work together as a group and access inter-professional training.

- Developing the skills of active listening, negotiation and compromise among multi-agency practitioners and staff within the educational setting.

- Appointing a multi-agency co-ordinator within the educational setting, or an ECM manager/director

- Developing clear inter-agency protocols for shared working and inter-agency service-level partnership delivery agreements.

- The existence of a strong genuine will and desire of practitioners from a range of services truly wanting to be involved in multi-agency partnership working, rather than being directed and compelled to engage in such activity.

- Producing a multi-agency directory for the educational setting, parents, carers, pupils and other stakeholders, which outlines different practitioners' roles, provides contact details, times of availability, and the location of the service or personnel.

- Holding multi-agency days in the educational setting, which enables members of the community, as well as other stakeholders to find out what support and services are offered to pupils and the wider community.

- Inviting multi-agency practitioners to parents' evenings, staff meetings and in-service education and training (INSET) days, in order to promote and publicize their achievements and services in working directly with children and young people in the educational setting.

The stages in the development of a multi-agency team

Bruce Tuckman's (1965) theory of team development and behaviour is helpful in assisting multi-agency practitioners to understand the four stages they work through, in order to become an effective team.

1. **Forming**: (clarifying roles and establishing relationships). Multi-agency team members:

   - will be introducing themselves and getting to know each other

   - will be trying to establish their individual identities

   - will be discussing the team's purpose

   - will be exploring the scope of the task

   - may be avoiding serious topics and feelings.

2. **Storming**: (resolving any tensions and disputes). This stage may involve:

   - multi-agency team members competing with one another

   - conflicting interests between team members arising, as the group becomes more focused on tasks

   - bending ideas, attitudes and beliefs to suit the team organization

   - questioning about who is responsible for what

   - discussing the multi-agency team's structure

   - conflicting views about structure, leadership, power and authority.

3. **Norming**: (starting to build the team identity). At this stage there will be:

- more cohesive multi-agency team relations

- a higher level of trust between multi-agency team members

- a greater focus on tasks

- accepted leadership of the multi-agency team

- a creative flow of information to inform the tasks.

4. **Performing**: (the multi-agency team has a shared vision, and it knows clearly what it is doing and achieves its goals). At this stage:

- multi-agency team members show a high level of dependence on one another

- there are deeper relationships between people

- the multi-agency team becomes good at problem-solving and there is more experimentation

- individual team members become more self-confident

- the multi-agency team is at its most productive

- team members review what they are doing
  (adapted from ContinYou, 2005b: 75).

Points to remember

- Educational settings cannot improve the wider ECM well-being of children and young people alone.
- Working in partnership with front-line multi-agency practitioners enables educational settings to focus on their core role of teaching and learning.
- Collaborative multi-agency partnership working promotes the sharing of skills, knowledge, expertise and ideas between practitioners.
- Every Child Matters is the 'gel' that holds partnership working together.

Further activities

The following questions, based on aspects covered in this chapter, are designed to enable staff from within the educational setting, in partnership with front-line practitioners from multi-agencies, working directly with pupils, to discuss and identify the benefits and challenges of collaborative partnership working in the context of the setting, and agree on positive ways forward to overcome any potential challenges.

- How is the educational setting you work in responding to, and being affected by, the implementation of Every Child Matters?

- What are the implications of Every Child Matters for the multi-agency front-line practitioners working with pupils in the educational setting?

Table 2.4   External service/agency information sheet

Name of organization:	
Profile:	
Address:	

Contact details:
Person:
Telephone: Fax:
Email: Website:

Opening/contact times:	

Services offered:

One-to-one support		Practical support	
Group support		Advice/information	
Outreach		Other	
Interpretation		Gender/ethnic specific	

Referral procedures:

Other information:

Sources: CEDC/ContinYou, 2003

 Photocopiable:

1. Do we share the same values and aspirations?

   ☐ There is a common vision that is set down and interpreted in similar ways between stakeholders.

   ☐ The full range of stakeholders have been involved through effective planning processes in developing the vision.

2. Do we have agreed priorities for significant policy and service shifts?

   ☐ There is a common interpretation of where and how services are currently succeeding and/or failing to meet children and young people's needs and wishes.

   ☐ There is agreement over the significant service changes that the partnership is designed to help achieve.

   ☐ The necessary links are in place with other planning processes to ensure policy and service changes are linked to the mainstream.

   ☐ Outcome criteria have been established to show whether changes have led to positive outcomes for children and young people.

3. Is there a willingness to explore new service options?

   ☐ Partners are willing to open up all aspects of service and practice to scrutiny through best value and user-led reviews.

   ☐ There is a culture of innovation and positive risk-taking in terms of service planning and design.

4. Is there agreement about the boundaries of the partnership?

   ☐ Resources are aligned with administrative and/or geographical boundaries in order that they can be shared flexibly.

   ☐ Boundaries with other services are agreed and clear.

5. Are we clear and comfortable with who will be responsible for what within the team partnership?

   ☐ It is clear where commissioning responsibility rests.

   ☐ There is a common definition and understanding of commissioning.

   ☐ There is a shared understanding of the nature of person-centred planning, care management and assessment, and of who is responsible for which aspects.

☐ The nature of the relationship between commissioners and providers of services is mutually acceptable.

☐ The role of service users in decision-making is clear and acceptable to all.

6. Is there confidence that each party's resource commitment is clear and open?

☐ Each party is confident and accepts that the resources committed to the partnership fully reflect the partners' contributions in reality.

☐ Any disagreements about past financial issues have been put behind you.

☐ Financial systems are robust enough to monitor and track resource commitments.

7. Is there effective, committed leadership to the partnership vision?

☐ Key senior players understand the issues and implications around partnership and are committed to its development.

☐ Senior officers are able and willing to make the time and space to build partnership working into their organizational agendas.

☐ Key practitioners are committed to a multi-professional way of working.

8. Are there people with time and capacity to take forward the partnership agenda?

☐ One or more individuals have been given a clear brief to lead on partnership development.

☐ Partnership is an integral part of everyone's work and job description.

9. Is there trust, openness and good will between key players?

☐ Key players at all levels in the organization are able and willing to work together constructively.

☐ There are strategies in place for managing and addressing difficult relationships.

☐ Time and opportunity is being built into working practices to allow people to get to know and understand each other's agendas.

(*Source*: DH, 2002: 17–9)

Figure 2.4   Checklist for building the multi-agency team

Photocopiable:

Effective Multi-Agency Partnerships, Sage Publications © Rita Cheminais, 2009

- What does each key practitioner from within the educational setting, in addition to those from multi-agencies, bring to the collaborative partnership, that enhances the learning and well-being outcomes of pupils?

- What benefit does each front-line multi-agency practitioner hope to achieve from working with the educational setting?

- How have you made clear the benefits that collaborative multi-agency partnership working brings, to the different stakeholders?

- What do front-line multi-agency practitioners expect from the others they collaboratively work with, in the educational setting?

- What are the views of pupils, and their parents/carers about the benefits and challenges that multi-agency service provision brings to them, and the educational setting?

- Are there any dangers to increased multi-agency partnership working? If so, what are these?

- What are the main barriers and challenges partners face in multi-agency working within the educational setting?

- What joint solution focused approaches are you taking in order to remove, and/or significantly reduce these barriers and challenges?

Further information

The following websites have downloadable resources which can help to support the aspects covered in this chapter.

www.nfer.ac.uk/publications/annual-survey-of-trends.cfm   NFER (2006) *How Is the Every Child Matters Agenda Affecting Schools? Annual Survey of Trends in Education.*

www.nfer.ac.uk/publications/annual-survey-of-trends-2007/ecmcollaborationprinted.pdf   NFER *How Is the Every Child Matters Agenda Affecting Schools? Annual Survey of Trends in Education.*

www.gtce.org.uk/publications/pub_policy/everychildmatters/?sort=dateDESC   *GTC document entitled, HM Government: Children's Workforce Strategy*

Update – Spring 2007. Building a World-Class Workforce for Children, Young People and Families.

http://lmscontent.ncsl.org.uk/ECM/   *NCSL/TDA report entitled, Understanding the Reasons Why Schools Do or Do Not Fully Engage with the ECM/ES Agenda.*

Do not forget to also visit the Sage website (www.sagepub.co.uk/cheminais) for downloadable resources to use with this chapter.

3

How to Operate and Manage Productive Multi-Agency Partnership Working

> **This chapter covers:**
>
> - **The building of relationships within the multi-agency team**
> - **The operation of a multi-agency partnership**
> - **Developing a multi-agency partnership agreement**
> - **Managing conflict and change**
> - **Factors to consider when seeking potential partners for the team**
> - **The multi-agency managed models of leadership**

This chapter is useful to leaders and managers setting up multi-agency teams.

Building relationships within the multi-agency team

How to operate and manage effective multi-agency partnership working is immensely challenging in terms of the extensive time needed for co-ordination, collaboration and partnership building. However, it is very rewarding when the efforts of multi-agency teamwork can be seen in improved outcomes for children and young people.

When you reflect on what has been the main key factor that has made multi-agency partnership working successful, it has to be the quality of the relationships that have been established between the different practitioners within the multidisciplinary team.

One headteacher commented on multi-agency working in an extended school: 'At the end of the day you can put all the structures in, but if the relationships aren't there they don't mean a thing. It's how it's done on a one-to-one basis that is absolutely paramount' (Coleman, 2006: 26).

Building good relationships within the multi-agency team are fostered through higher-order ways of getting practitioners to work together, for example, joint meetings, joint training activities, joint report writing, joint preparation of proposals and bids for funding, and joint evaluations.

Relationships between practitioners in the multi-agency team are also strengthened when:

- internal support is gained from other colleagues

- there is a high level of trust between practitioners in the team

- good communication and networking exists across all the different agencies

- a common language is used between practitioners

- practitioners within the team listen to each other and value each other's opinions

- practitioners receive honest feedback in the team, and are offered two positive feedbacks for every one negative feedback

- practitioners jointly adopt a solution-focused approach to problem-solving.

In October 2005, at Our Partnership – Your Conference, delegates proposed the following recommendations for gaining greater commitment and ownership in multi-agency partnerships.

- Develop relationships and trust.

- Have joint agendas.

- Have transparency in decision-making.

- Have a clear shared vision.

- Have agreement on partners' roles.

- Have a willingness to compromise.

- Have clear agreed objectives.

- Develop respect.

- Make sure the right people are involved.

- Ensure contribution from all partners.

- Have a recognition of roles and boundaries.

- Have an agreed purpose and vision.

- Develop momentum by focusing on quick wins.

- Agree common goals and win-wins.

- Agree expectations.

- Agree resource implications and timescales.

Developing a multi-agency partnership agreement

It is good practice if senior leaders and managers of the educational setting establish a written multi-agency partnership agreement. The agreement needs to cover:

- what you intend to achieve

- how you are going to manage and resource the multi-agency partnership

- how you are going to deal with any potential conflicts within the partnership.

The multi-agency partnership agreement for the educational setting needs to include:

1. Aims and objectives

    - brief explanation on what is the purpose of the multi-agency partnership

    - indication of what added value the multi-agency team will achieve

    - a statement on how the team will determine success.

2. Strategy and activities

    - stating how the multi-agency practitioners in the team will realize the team's goals.

3. Membership and decision-making

    - indication of what the basis for membership of the multi-agency partnership should be

    - specifying how decisions will be taken within the partnership.

4. Management and operation of the partnership

    - stating what the main issues to be addressed are and an indication of how they will be handled by the team

    - specifying what principles/ground rules will govern and guide the multi-agency partnership in the educational setting

    - an indication of who on the senior leadership team they will report to

Figure 3.1   Checklist for operating a multi-agency team in an educational setting

☐   There exists a clear vision and purpose for working collaboratively.

☐   There is a written partnership agreement giving the terms of reference for the operation of the multi-agency team.

☐   Clear roles and responsibilities exist which prevent overlap.

☐   Practitioners in the team are given time to get to know each other through joint training and team building activities.

☐   Practitioners in the team meet formally every month to review their work and plan for future developments/improvements in team-working.

☐   Line management is clear as to who oversees the work of practitioners, while they are working within an educational setting.

☐   There is a budget available for capacity building within the team.

☐   ICT facilities are available to support information sharing.

☐   The multi-agency team has a room/base in the educational setting.

☐   There is a senior member of staff who acts as a point of contact for the multi-agency team, within the educational setting.

☐   There are clear procedures and protocols existing for the referral of children to, and out of, the multi-agency team.

☐   Procedures for conflict resolution between team workers is in place.

☐   Reflective practice is encouraged between practitioners within the team.

☐   Effective systems are in place to monitor, evaluate and report on the multi-agency team's activities and outcomes.

- an indication of how practitioner responsibilities will be shared and divided up

- explanation of how and when performance of the team and its members will be reviewed.

5. Resources

- a description of how the multi-agency partnership is resourced and kept sustainable.

6. Information

- an explanation of what information will be shared between practitioners in the multi-agency team partnership, and why it has to be shared.

7. Conflict avoidance/dispute resolution

- a brief explanation describing how any disputes within the multi-agency will be dealt with.

Managing conflict

A range of strategies can be used to resolve any conflict that may arise within a multi-agency team. The key to managing conflict successfully is choosing and using the most appropriate strategy that best fits the situation.

The main conflict management strategies are outlined in Table 3.1.

Managing change

There are a number of popular models for managing change which senior leaders can utilize, in relation to building and developing multi-agency partnership working, in the educational setting. These are described in Table 3.2.

Change is a developmental process that aims to improve practice and introduce new policies and functions. It frequently entails practitioners working in a new way, moving away from familiar practices, and challenging existing beliefs, assumptions and values. The Every Child Matters Change for Children programme (DfES, 2004a) aims to improve the ECM outcomes for children and young people with additional needs. This core ECM aim provides the justification for the change in what the multi-agency team does, or how it operates. As one headteacher commented: 'It helps to be able to point to shared objectives via ECM with other agencies and services. It gives a clarity of purpose to the partnerships' (Kendal et al., 2007: 37).

Every Child Matters clearly acts as a catalyst for change because it provides the impetus, status and motivation to integrate services in order to achieve better outcomes for children and young people.

The following tasks relating to change are useful to undertake individually, as well as together, as a whole multi-agency team in an educational setting.

Table 3.1   Conflict management strategies

Conflict strategy	Features	Application
Forcing	Using formal authority or other power to satisfy your concerns relating to the practitioner you are in conflict with	When time is pressurized and an important issue has arisen that requires a quick resolution, forcing becomes necessary. There will be a need to repair the relationship after using the forcing strategy
Accommodating	Allowing the other party to satisfy their concerns while neglecting your own	Useful approach to use when conflict is over a fairly unimportant issue. It offers a quick way to resolve conflict without straining your relationship with the other party
Avoiding	Not paying attention to the conflict and not taking any action to resolve it	Useful approach to use for situations where there is a clear advantage to waiting to resolve the conflict. Avoiding is also useful to use if you are too busy with more important concerns, and if your relationship with the other party is not important. Avoiding is a poor strategy to choose if the issue or the relationship between the parties is important
Compromising	Attempting to resolve a conflict by identifying a solution that is partially satisfactory to both parties, but completely satisfactory to neither	Useful when dealing with moderately important issues. It can lead to quick solutions, but it does not foster innovation
Collaborating	Co-operating with the other party to understand their concerns and expressing your concerns in an effort to find a mutually and completely satisfactory solution (win-win)	Useful approach to adopt for handling conflicts over very important issues. Collaboration promotes creative problem-solving. It also helps to foster mutual respect and rapport. Collaboration can be quite a time-consuming process

Task 3.1: Changing practice

On the postcard provided (Figure 3.3), each write down one aspect of your work/practice with children and young people in the educational setting, that you wish to change in the next month, which will lead to an improved ECM outcome and will result in far more effective multi-agency partnership working.

Table 3.2   Models of change

Fullan's model	Kotter's model	NRT model
Five-stage model	Eight-stage model	Five-stage model
1. **Moral purpose** – the values and vision (ECM), helps participants to see that change will make a difference for the better 2. **Understanding change** – sharing the big picture; developing and building capacity for change; team-building; encouraging the 'buy-in' to change 3. **Relationship-building** – developing emotional intelligence and being sensitive to the needs of others 4. **Knowledge creation and sharing** – defining the learning and well-being community; raising awareness, developing skills; creating and sharing new knowledge 5. **Coherence-making** – encouraging some creativity to prevent stagnation; avoiding initiative overload by prioritizing	1. **Establishing a sense of urgency** – identifying and discussing potential crisis and major opportunities 2. **Form a powerful, guiding coalition** – assemble a group who will work together as a team to lead the change effort 3. **Create a vision** – to direct the change effort with strategies for achieving the vision 4. **Communicate the vision and strategies** – by a range of methods; teach new ways of working through guiding 5. **Empower others to act on the vision** – get rid of obstacles to change; change systems or structures that undermine the vision; encourage risk-taking, creativity and innovation 6. **Plan and create short-term wins** – visible performance improvements that are recognized and rewarded 7. **Consolidate improvements and produce still more change** – by recruiting, promoting and developing credible employees acting as change agents, who can implement the vision and introduce new project themes 8. **Institutionalize new approaches** – disseminate and articulate the successful change; ensure leadership development and succession	1. **Understand and appreciate** the reason for change; starting to address issues; developing mutual respect 2. **Discover** that this change is bigger than first thought, but there is commitment to it 3. **Deepen** understanding of change; it is tough but a solution can be found, and there is greater clarity 4. **Develop and experience change** – there is a strategy and a plan for future success. There is openness existing among participants and stakeholders 5. **Deliver** – some issues have been resolved and a way forward has been found. A high level of trust exists

Figure 3.2   Checklist for managing change for multi-agency collaboration

☐ Share the moral purpose – e.g. ECM outcomes make change necessary and they shape the vision and mission.

☐ Help others to understand the change process – share the big picture and promote working in new and different ways, avoiding initiative overload.

☐ Adopt a team approach, building trust between partners from within and outside the educational setting.

☐ Redesign jobs and roles for staff in the educational setting, to maximize their strengths in supporting multi-agency partnership working and activities.

☐ Demonstrate emotional intelligence through being sensitive to the needs of others.

☐ Look for new partners to build capacity for ECM.

☐ Develop more flexible organizational structures responsive to the needs of children and their parents/carers.

☐ Develop a learning culture and a learning community where practitioners learn from others.

☐ Achieve coherence and connectedness – avoid taking too much on at once.

☐ Foster a solution-focused approach.

☐ Adopt the wider view to become an outward facing organization – making a difference locally by developing a shared local commitment and building relationships.

 Photocopiable:
Effective Multi-Agency Partnerships, Sage Publications © Rita Cheminais, 2009

Figure 3.3 Changing practice postcard

The one aspect of my work/practice I will change in the next month is:

The reason why I will change this practice is because:

 Photocopiable:
Effective Multi-Agency Partnerships, Sage Publications © Rita Cheminais, 2009

Discuss this change with another member of the team from a different service.

Display all the postcards to enable the full team to view the changes.

Task 3.2: What helps to effect change?

This task is for multi-agency teams to work on initially individually, then in a pair, and finally, as a whole team.

(a) Individually, write down on a piece of flip-chart paper something you have changed in the past two months in your multi-agency working practice.

(b) Then write down what/who helped you to make the change happen.

(c) Where appropriate, write down any barriers that you met, which hampered or slowed the rate of change.

(d) Discuss and share your change experience with another member of your multi-agency team, and then listen to their change experience.

(e) What are the overall lessons to be learnt about change in a multi-agency partnership?

Task 3.3: Managing change in the multi-agency team

As a whole multi-agency team:

(a) Discuss and agree upon one priority for improving the team's multi-agency partnership working.

(b) Using the template provided on flip-chart paper (Figure 3.4), write down the agreed priority for improving the team's multi-agency partnership working in the central circle number 1.

(c) Working around the template, write in the actions and support required to meet and address the identified team priority.

Task 3.4: Life cycle stages of a multi-agency partnership

See Table 3.3.

Ten steps to the multi-agency partnership management process

When senior leaders and managers in an educational setting are deciding how to manage the multi-agency team on the site, there are some useful questions to consider.

1. What is the core purpose of the multi-agency partnership and what needs to be achieved by when?

2. How do you know the multi-agency partnership can realistically provide what is required in the given time?

Figure 3.4 Managing change in a multi-agency team

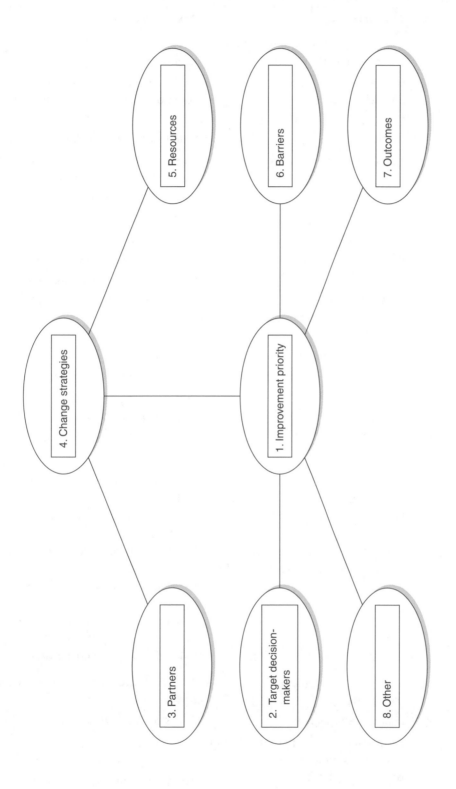

Table 3.3   The life cycle of a multi-agency partnership

At what stage is your multi-agency team at on the partnership life cycle?

Stage	Characteristics	Action/solutions
1. Forming	Common cause arising from shared interests, opportunities and threats	Create opportunities for people to get to know each other
	Early enthusiasm – new challenges, new relationships	Encourage partners to focus on a common vision, and the difference they want to make together
	Exploring what's needed, what's possible	Define tasks and tangible outcomes
	Nature of commitments is unclear	Shepherd the process of building the partnership agenda – including through the use of research
		Ensure neutral meeting ground
2. Frustration	Partners feel 'in a fog'	Revisit the common ground – allow time to redefine issues, purpose
	Disputes or tension over priorities and methods	Maximize opportunities for practical involvement. Implement actions which demonstrate progress
	Individuals questioning purpose of the partnership and reasons for being there	Encourage open expression and constructive disagreement
	Hidden agendas influencing what partners do	Clarify benefits to individual partners
	Doubts about what each other brings to the partnership	Promote mutual appreciation of what each other can contribute
	Partners competing for credit and control	Fix the problem, not the blame
3. Functioning	Renewed vision and focus	Agree clear objectives, responsibilities, success measures
	Progress through joint project teams	Establish principles/protocols for collaboration
	Partners talk in terms of 'we' not 'you'	
	Clear roles and responsibilities	Encourage shared leadership and accountability
	Full accountability to each other for actions	Develop common methods and quality standards
		Seek learning consciously through cross-partner project teams, joint training and reviewing activities
4. Flying	Successful achievement of partnership goals	Anticipate future challenges and build partner capacity to respond
	Shared leadership	Take stock of how well the group is performing
	Partners changing what they do and how they do it to achieve partnership objectives	Keep working at communications
	Trust and mutual respect	Avoid any unnecessary partnership working
	Partnership priorities central to partner activities	Ask: does the partnership still serve its purpose?

Table 3.3   (Continued)

Stage	Characteristics	Action/solutions
		Ensure that all partners are getting the benefits they expect
		Continue to celebrate success
5. Failing	Disengagement, lack of commitment, recurrent tensions, breakdown or frittering away of relationships	Go back to stage 1

3. Is there anyone missing from the multi-agency team, that is, potential partners who are needed?

4. Who, of the major practitioners (existing or potential), will bring the greatest gains to the multi-agency partnership?

5. Which multi-agency working team structure (co-located or virtual) will bring the greatest gains to children/young people in the educational setting?

6. What do the multi-agency practitioners require from their service users in order to enable them to perform their role effectively?

7. What is the best way to manage any different interests and power relationships existing within the multi-agency team?

8. How will you identify and agree some 'quick wins' for the team?

9. How will you bring together and maximize the different multi-agency practitioners working cultures?

10. How will the work of the multi-agency partnership be evaluated?

Eight features of an effective multi-agency partnership

1. Practitioners in the team can demonstrate **real results through collaboration.**

2. **Common interest** (ECM outcomes) supersedes practitioner interest.

3. Team practitioners **use 'we'** when talking about practitioner matters.

4. Practitioners in the team are **mutually accountable** for tasks and outcomes.

5. Practitioners **share** responsibilities and rewards.

6. Practitioners strive to develop and maintain **trust**.

7. Practitioners are **willing to change** what they do and how they do it.

8. Practitioners **seek to improve** how the partnership performs (LGpartnerships – Smarter partnerships, www.lgpartnerships.com/howhealthy.asp).

Clarifying roles and responsibilities within the multi-agency team

Use the following questions to reflect upon and review the multi-agency partnership team roles and responsibilities.

• Is this something we need to do?

• Who is responsible?

• Is it a shared responsibility?

• Is the responsibility clearly allocated?

• Do we need to carry out the responsibility more? Better?

• What action is needed? By whom, and by when?

One practitioner commented in the Barnardo's research into inter-agency working in children's centres: 'We make assumptions about what we can all do. Clarity in work roles and responsibilities needs to be agreed from the start of a team working together' (McInnes, 2007: 25).

The four 'M's' for reviewing the operation of the multi-agency team

• Is what you have set out to do **meaningful**?

• Will you feel **motivated** to work towards the goals set?

• Is what you set out to do **manageable**?

• Is what you've set out to do **measurable**?

Multi-agency benchmark self-assessment

Table 3.4 is a quick and useful self-assessment activity for practitioners to undertake individually. It can be anonymous, but helpful to request that the practitioners indicate which service/agency they work for. Senior leaders and managers within the education setting can review the findings, and make any necessary changes to improve the effectiveness of the multi-agency team.

Table 3.4 Multi-agency benchmark self-assessment

	Benchmark descriptor	Yes, working well	Needs improving
1	Team practitioners share a **common vision** of the difference they want to make and the direction to take		
2	Team practitioners focus on partnership **added value**: how they can achieve more or better results through collaboration		
3	Team practitioners are **willing to make changes** to achieve shared goals		
4	Team practitioners **facilitate partnership working** and engender support within their own organizations or interest grouping		
5	Team practitioners' objectives are **aligned** in a common direction, e.g. ECM outcomes		

Source: LGpartnerships – Smarter partnerships (www.lgpartnerships.com/diggingdeeper/leadership.asp)

 Photocopiable:
Effective Multi-Agency Partnerships, Sage Publications © Rita Cheminais, 2009

Factors to consider when seeking potential practitioners to join the multi-agency team

- What can potential practitioners offer to the work of the team, that is different, and that will add value?

- What would make joining your multi-agency team attractive to potential practitioners?

- Have you undertaken sufficient background research into the previous successes, achievements, credibility and quality of the potential practitioner(s)?

- What do the potential practitioners hope to achieve by joining your multi-agency team?

- Have you sought the views of the existing team members, and those of any other stakeholders about inviting the potential practitioner to join the multi-agency team.

- Is the potential practitioner the best option, or are there others who could provide what you are looking for to enhance the work of the multi-agency team?

- How can you be certain that the potential practitioner will be committed to the vision and aims of the multi-agency partnership?

- What additional resources will the potential practitioner bring to the multi-agency team?

- How can you be sure that they have the time to deliver the service you require?

Once you have found out all the answers to the above questions, and you feel happy about the new practitioner joining the multi-agency team, you may wish to issue them with a formal partnership commitment agreement, as shown in Figure 3.5.

Developing the skills for multi-agency partnership working

Smarter Partnerships provide a very useful detailed self-assessment tool to enable leaders, managers and individual multi-agency practitioners to look in greater depth at the skills required to enhance partnership working. The tool focuses on four main partnership aspects: leadership, trust, learning and managing for performance (in relation to managing change). Table 3.5 provides a summary of the key skills required for each partnership aspect.

Collaborative working survey

The NCSL provide a good model survey for multi-agency collaborative working (Table 3.6) on their ECM Leadership Direct website. The survey is designed to be

Name of new practitioner: _____

Service: _____

Date of joining multi-agency team: _____

Contact information

Address:

Telephone:

Email:

Role being provided:

Requirements to perform role:

Storage requirements for equipment/resources:

Time requirements to deliver the service:

Funding contributions, where appropriate:

Professional development/training requirements:

Figure 3.5   Model partnership commitment agreement

used in multi-agency or multidisciplinary teams who are working together on a permanent basis in an educational setting, or who are working collaboratively on a time-limited project.

The survey acts as a diagnostic tool to stimulate team discussion on the positive factors and tensions impacting on their collaborative effort. The themes in the collaborative working survey are based on practitioner experience and action research. The themes reflect the complexities of collaborative working, that may need to be managed.

Leaders of educational settings and multi-agency team leaders can use the collaborative working survey to check on the effectiveness of the team's collaborative effort. The survey will help to identify what is working well, and what is causing tensions in the multi-agency partnership.

The survey can be repeated over time to assess the development and progress in collaborative working of the multi-agency team within the educational setting.

Table 3.5 Skills and knowledge audit for multi-agency partnership working

Aspect	Skills and knowledge	Personal	Team	Partnership
Leadership skills	Coalition-building			
	Vision and consensus-building			
	Communicating			
	Consultation			
	Managing change			
	Delegating			
	Influencing			
	Negotiating roles and contributions			
	Assertiveness			
Leadership knowledge of	Needs and opportunities which provide the basis for common ground			
	Policy and funding developments			
	Practitioner roles, contributions, constraints, motivations			
	Potential benefits, costs and risks for individual practitioners			
	Forms of partnership added value			
	Interdependencies between practitioner activities			

(Continued)

Table 3.5 (Continued)

Aspect	Skills and knowledge	Personal	Team	Partnership
Leadership knowledge of	How to overcome barriers to practitioner engagement and commitment			
	Use of performance management systems to reinforce partnership			
Trust skills	Building robust relationships			
	Managing expectations			
	Promoting dialogue			
	Listening			
	Empathy			
	Managing disagreement and conflict			
	Giving constructive feedback			
	Managing communications			
	Coping with the unfamiliar and the unexpected			
Trust knowledge	Group dynamics			
	Cultures, values and ways of working with others			
	How partners can hinder the contribution of others			

(Continued)

Table 3.5 (Continued)

Aspect	Skills and knowledge	Personal	Team	Partnership
	Forms of partnership agreement			
	Methods to build the capacity of practitioners and the team	,		
Learning skills	Problem solving/creative thinking			
	Systems thinking			
	Networking			
	Diagnosing performance issues			
Learning knowledge	Benchmarking and process mapping for analysing and comparing performance			
	Partnership review and evaluation			
	How to promote learning in partnerships/groups			
	Learning needs analysis			
	Facilitation techniques			
	Powers, motivations and constraints potential of other practitioners/partners			
	Nature of implications of the partnership life cycle			
Managing for performance – skills	Negotiating			

(Continued)

Table 3.5 (Continued)

Aspect	Skills and knowledge	Personal	Team	Partnership
	Entrepreneurial			
	Setting objectives and performance measures			
	Project team-building			
	Project planning and project management			
Managing for performance – knowledge	Partnership structures			
	Accountability mechanisms			
	Functions required for successful performance			
	Co-ordination methods			
	Managing meetings			
	Partnership evaluation methods			
	Sources of finance and in-kind resources			
	Ways of making better use of resources			
	Collaborative use of ICT (for information sharing)			

Source: Local government national training organization (IGNTO) – Smarter Partnerships and Educe Limited (www.lgpartnerships.com)

 Photocopiable:

Effective Multi-Agency Partnerships, Sage Publications © Rita Cheminais, 2009

Table 3.6   Collaborative working survey

Please rate your level of agreement with the statements below by circling the score which describes your collaborative effort	Rating: 1 = strongly agree 2 = agree 3 = disagree 4 = strongly disagree			
1 We have developed common aims	1	2	3	4
2 We have developed shared compatible aims	1	2	3	4
3 There is good communication between members of the team	1	2	3	4
4 There is clarity about each member's role and who/what they represent	1	2	3	4
5 There are deepening bonds of commitment and determination between members to achieve the aims	1	2	3	4
6 Members are prepared to compromise in the interests of the common aims	1	2	3	4
7 We have developed effective working processes which help get things done	1	2	3	4
8 There is accountability between members for following through on decisions which have been agreed	1	2	3	4
9 The leadership of the collaboration enacts principles, democracy and equality to empower everyone to take an active role	1	2	3	4
10 Members share resources	1	2	3	4
11 Members do not undermine each other or behave in ways which have a negative impact on others	1	2	3	4
12 Members trust each other to behave in ways which show respect	1	2	3	4
13 Power (personal and role) is used wisely to avoid over control by any one member	1	2	3	4
14 Due to working together we make faster, better decisions	1	2	3	4
15 Members share information and knowledge	1	2	3	4
16 Members are recognized and appreciated for their contribution	1	2	3	4
17 There is productive output as a result of our collaboration	1	2	3	4
18 The synergy achieved through collaboration makes things happen that wouldn't or couldn't otherwise happen	1	2	3	4
	Individual total			

Source: (NCSL, ECM Leadership Direct website – collaborative working survey (http://lmscontent.ncsl.org.uk/ECM/index.cfm?n=810), 2007

Administering the survey

- Give each member of the multi-agency team a copy of the survey to complete, rating the current collaborative working arrangements.

- Collect the surveys and collate the scores, identifying strengths and tensions.

- Share the overall findings with the team, and discuss what the team can do differently to achieve greater collaborative advantage.

The multi-agency managed model of leadership

PriceWaterhouseCoopers LLP were commissioned by the Department for Education and Skills (DfES) to undertake an independent study into school leadership, during 2006. The findings from the research found that the multi-agency managed model of leadership had arisen as a result of the Every Child Matters agenda (DfES, 2007).

This model of leadership in schools acknowledges the important link between children's educational and social outcomes. It is an outward-looking and inter-agency focused leadership model, which is becoming essential where schools form a federation, collaborating and sharing resources between schools. The model entails a greater degree of multi-agency working and a more diverse children's workforce being based on an educational settings premises. It involves teaching staff and practitioners from other agencies working together as part of the school's leadership team. This greater diversity in the senior leadership team results in dedicated directors for areas such as inclusion, teaching and learning, ECM, business development and human resources being appointed. The multi-agency managed model of leadership is beginning to see the introduction of the chief executive combined with a lead practitioner model, on similar lines to the National Health Service (NHS) leadership model, in Figure 3.6, which illustrates the skills, knowledge and personal qualities required for the multi-agency leadership role in an educational setting.

In the multi-agency managed model of leadership, members of staff from other agencies and services, that is, health and social services, can sit either on the senior leadership team or on the governing body/management board of the educational setting. There can also be a dedicated post with specific ECM-related responsibilities.

The multi-agency managed model of leadership has implications for headteachers/ senior leaders. These are:

- having responsibility for a much more diverse workforce on the educational setting's site

- having to develop a common professional language

- establishing lines of accountability for different groups of staff, linked to clear performance management arrangements

- negotiating and monitoring the delivery of services provided by the private sector or other organizations.

The advantages and disadvantages of the multi-agency managed model of leadership are summarized in Table 3.7.

Figure 3.6 The NHS leadership model 2002

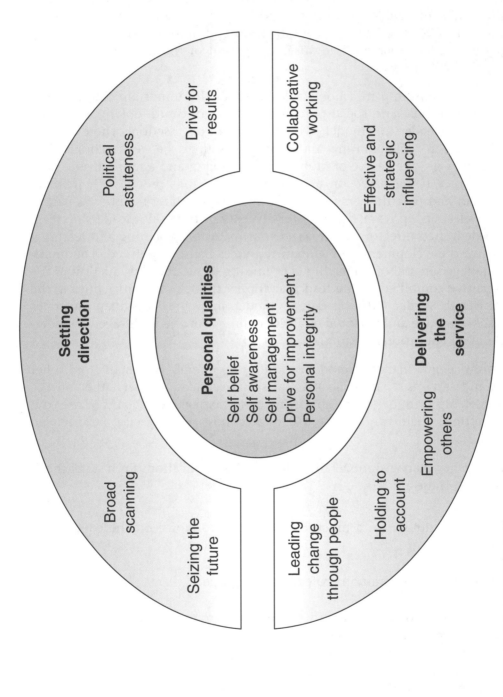

Setting direction

Political astuteness

Drive for results

Broad scanning

Seizing the future

Personal qualities

Self belief
Self awareness
Self management
Drive for improvement
Personal integrity

Collaborative working

Effective and strategic influencing

Delivering the service

Leading change through people

Holding to account

Empowering others

Source: DfES 2007: 40, Crown Copyright, 2007

Photocopiable:

Effective Multi-Agency Partnerships, Sage Publications © Rita Cheminais, 2009

Table 3.7   The advantages and disadvantages of the multi-agency managed model of leadership

Potential advantages/benefits	Potential disadvantages/constraints
• Assists in developing future leaders through increased inter-agency working • Potential to raise standards and achievement • Potential to improve attendance and well-being of pupils • Improved relationships and communication between different children's services • Earlier and more rapid intervention for children with additional needs • Greater access to welfare and other services for children and their families • Greater parental commitment to and involvement in the educational setting • Improved relations with the wider community and increased consultation in the locality • Creates an effective transition for children between home and work • Demonstrates empowerment through distributed leadership	• Unclear accountability issues • Confusion over roles • Financial and insurance issues • Human resources issues, e.g. legal implications • Cultural and operational differences between multi-agency teams, e.g. professional terminology, different administrative requirements • Sustainability of funding for specific initiatives • Availability of staff if some are working on multi-agency teams • Buildings management and premises management and negotiating access to the educational setting's site • May require a cultural change in some educational settings • Training and development for the entire educational setting's workforce

Source: DfES, 2007: 67

The skills needed by leaders in educational settings for ECM

Every Child Matters requires school leaders to be much more politically astute and outward facing, with a good understanding of the local context. Leaders of educational settings require the following:

• negotiation skills

• change management skills

• brokerage ability

• interpersonal skills

• team-building capacity

• risk management

• financial acumen

• contextual literacy.

> **Points to remember**
>
> - The quality of the relationship between the different practitioners in the multi-agency team is what determines a successful partnership.
> - A written partnership agreement setting out the terms of reference for the operation of the multi-agency team is essential.
> - Having shared ECM objectives within the multi-agency team helps to give clarity of purpose to the partnerships.
> - Developing a learning culture and a learning community is crucial to ensuring multi-agency practitioners learn from each other.

Further activities

The following questions, based on aspects covered in this chapter, are designed to enable senior leaders within an educational setting, in partnership with front-line practitioners from the multi-agency team to reflect on how they could further improve the operation and management of the multi-agency partnership.

- How will you continue to build good relationships in the multi-agency team in order to improve service delivery?

- How can the multi-agency team ensure that their partnership working is adding value?

- What longer-term outcomes does the multi-agency team seek to achieve?

- What additional support does the multi-agency team require in order to achieve the longer-term outcomes?

- How can you ensure that the key teaching staff from the educational setting obtain the necessary quality time to get together with all the multi-agency team practitioners to review their joint working and progress?

- How will you create opportunities for joint learning to occur between the multi-agency team practitioners and the staff in the educational setting?

- Who else do you need to work with, external to the educational setting, who can help you and the multi-agency team to further improve the ECM outcomes for children and young people?

- Have you got sufficient administrative capacity to support the operation of multi-agency partnership working?

- How far do your organizational structures support the multi-agency activity?

- To what extent do partner organizations share a vision and common goal for the multi-agency activity?

- How integrated is the multi-agency team and how deeply into the structures and vision of the team does collaboration penetrate?

Further information

The following websites have downloadable resources which provide further information about the operation and management of multi-agency partnerships.

www.lgpartnerships.com   This website provides a wealth of information in relation to operating and managing effective partnerships. It offers several useful tools for exploring in greater depth the skills required for partnership working.

www.ourpartnership.org.uk   This website has useful information about operating a community partnership. The information is transferable and relevant to a multi-agency partnership.

www.everychildmatters.gov.uk/deliveringservices/multi-agencyworking   This government website provides information relating to the factors that lead to the successful operation of a multi-agency partnership.

http://lmscontent.ncsl.org.uk/ECM/   This NCSL website 'ECM Leadership Direct' provides a useful resource for school leaders on multi-agency partnerships and collaborative teamwork. It also offers guidance on running a Leading Challenge Workshop, where multi-agency collaboration and partnership working can be discussed in depth.

www.nao.org.uk/change_management_toolkit/index.htm   This website has lots of useful documents relating to managing change, covering topics such as addressing behaviour and culture, engaging stakeholders, and communication.

Do not forget to also visit the Sage website (www.sagepub.co.uk/cheminais) for downloadable resources to use with this chapter.

Developing Effective Team Around the Child Partnership Working

> **This chapter outlines:**
>
> - The origin, concept and principles of Team Around the Child (TAC)
> - The functions, features, benefits and challenges of TAC
> - Best practice research in gathering stakeholders views on TAC
> - Key elements of good practice in TAC
> - Practical activities for developing effective TAC partnerships

This chapter is useful for those leading and co-ordinating a TAC.

The origins of Team Around the Child

The concept of Team Around the Child is not new in terms of good professional practice. The original TAC was advocated by an independent consultant, Peter Limbrick, in 2001, who had experience of the process used with children with multiple and complex needs. The green paper *Every Child Matters*, which the government published in September 2003, (DfES, 2003), made reference to Team Around the Child.

The DfES's comment in *Every Child Matters: Change for Children* (2004a), reflects the requirements for an effective TAC approach: 'Delivering more integrated services requires new ways of working and significant cultural change for staff working within narrower professional and service-based boundaries. Easy and effective communication across current organisational and professional boundaries is a strong foundation for co-operation' (DfES, 2004a:17).

The subsequent Children Act 2004, recommended multi-agency collaborative partnership working as being an effective way of meeting the needs of children, young people and families with additional and more complex needs.

The definition and concept of Team Around the Child

According to the government, in their *Every Child Matters* glossary, Team Around the Child is a model of service provision in which a range of different practitioners come together to help and support an individual child. Peter Limbrick defined the TAC as being: 'an individualised and evolving team of the few practitioners who see the child and family on a regular basis to provide practical support in education, therapy and treatment' (Limbrick, 2005: 1). The needs-led approach suggests a group of professionals working together only when required to help in improving outcomes for a particular child or young person, for example, operating as a 'virtual' team, working with a range of different colleagues at different times to support particular children.

Team Around the Child is designed to be an uncomplicated, appealing, common-sense, easily understood and non-threatening concept for parents, children and practitioners alike.

Team Around the Child provides a local framework for joint multi-agency working that offers a structure which enables different practitioners to work together more effectively, in order to achieve quality outcomes. The TAC local framework applies to all practitioners working within universal, targeted and specialist provision across the statutory and voluntary sector. The TAC will manifest itself in different ways at different times for different children and young people.

The Team Around the Child may vary in size and composition, according to the needs of the child, ideally remaining small and manageable, for example, comprising three to six members. For example, a small team may comprise the parent of the child, a class teacher, the special educational needs co-ordinator (SENCO) and a psychologist. A larger TAC may include the family, a social worker, physiotherapist, occupational therapist, speech and language therapist, and a health visitor/community nurse. The TAC will be an evolving team of practitioners who see the child/young person and family on a regular basis to provide practical support, as well as those who are able to work directly with the child, young person and family. As the needs of the child change and the family's circumstances alter, the membership of the TAC will also change.

The TAC brings together professionals and practitioners who may not normally work directly with each other, but who all work with children and young people. The TAC requires professionals to work in a different way and to offer a range of successful support mechanisms. The team works together to plan co-ordinated support from agencies to address problems in a holistic way. The aim and purpose of the TAC is to reduce overlap and duplication in service provision, and to support a common way in which to deliver joined-up co-ordinated services locally, in order to address the root cause of the child's or young person's additional needs, which may relate to their behaviour, learning or health needs.

The TAC meetings support analysis, sense-making and problem-solving as professionals from different agencies come together with the parent(s) on equal terms to discuss needs and agree a co-ordinated approach to meeting those needs. The expected outcomes from an initial TAC meeting will be the production of an agreed Child and Family Plan, which sets out expectations from all workers, including the child and their family. A date for the next meeting will be set, to identify if the plan is meeting the child's needs.

Figure 4.1 Team Around the Child (TAC) pupil-friendly plan

Name of pupil: _____ Form/Class: _____

Date of birth: _____ Date of TAC meeting: _____

Name of people at the TAC meeting	Main comments about pupil progress and outcomes
1.	
2.	
3.	
4.	
5.	
6.	

Names of any people unable to attend the TAC meeting: _____

_____

Team Around the Child member	Next steps and action (What each person will do)
1.	
2.	
3.	
4.	
5.	
6.	

Pupil signature: _____

Lead professional name (print): _____

Lead professional signature: _____

Date of the next TAC meeting: _____

Photocopiable:
Effective Multi-Agency Partnerships, Sage Publications © Rita Cheminais, 2009

Figure 4.2 Team Around the Child questionnaire

Please answer the following questions as best you can, about the Team Around the Child (TAC) meeting you attended.

Name: _____ Date of TAC meeting: _____

Venue of TAC meeting: _____

✓ tick one box after each question that matches what you thought about the meeting.

1. Was the purpose of the TAC meeting made clear to you? ☐ YES ☐ NO
2. Did you feel able to give your views at the TAC meeting? ☐ YES ☐ NO
3. Did you feel your views were listened to by others? ☐ YES ☐ NO
4. Were your views noted and taken seriously by others? ☐ YES ☐ NO
5. Did you think the lead professional led the meeting well? ☐ YES ☐ NO
6. Do you feel OK about what the TAC plan next steps are? ☐ YES ☐ NO
7. Were you happy with the venue for the meeting? ☐ YES ☐ NO
8. Did you feel the TAC meeting went on for too long? ☐ YES ☐ NO
9. What could be done to make the next meeting better? (Please comment below)

_____

_____

_____

_____

10. Is there anything else you wish to comment on about the TAC meeting you have just attended? If so, please write your comments below.

_____

_____

_____

_____

Thank you for taking the time to complete this questionnaire.

Your views are important to us.
Please place your questionnaire in the post box in the main entrance of school.

 Photocopiable:

Effective Multi-Agency Partnerships, Sage Publications © Rita Cheminais, 2009

The principles of Team Around the Child

There are six key principles which guide the work of the TAC. These include:

- every child with additional and more complex needs having a practitioner known as the 'lead professional', who is responsible for co-ordinating service delivery

- well-co-ordinated delivery of support by all practitioners involved with the child, young person or family being present

- the family and multi-agency practitioners having a clear assessment and record of needs, strengths, and actions that can be shared, built on and reviewed

- the child, young person, parent and family's engagement viewed as being essential to the success of the TAC approach

- TAC practice supporting and valuing the cultural needs of the child, young person and family

- TAC promoting and supporting the early identification of need and early multi-agency/multidisciplinary intervention and preventative work.

The functions of the Team Around the Child

The functions of the TAC are to:

- agree the needs of the child, young person and family

- agree the family support needs

- support the child to meet their identified needs

- arrange, as necessary, additional support based on a common assessment, which provides a pathway to targeted and specialist services

- review the support given to the child and family

- report, as required, on the progress of the child, young person and family

- identify gaps in service provision and inform future planning and commissioning of local services.

The essential features of an effective Team Around the Child

An effective Team Around the Child:

- is supportive and encouraging to all members

- gives all members an equal voice

- is able to arrive at collective agreements

- acknowledges different viewpoints

- is able to negotiate workable solutions.

The benefits of the Team Around the Child approach

The main benefits of the TAC are as follows:

- greater efficiency and effectiveness in multi-agency working and service provision

- closer engagement with service users and the local community

- improved access to services delivered locally to meet the needs of children, young people and families, for example, in children's centres, extended schools, general practitioner (GP) surgeries, health centres and joint service centres

- preventative multi-agency services targeted at removing barriers to children and young people's learning, enabling them to raise their attainment, improve attendance, and reduce exclusions and antisocial behaviour

- act as a driver for cultural and organizational change to ensure the implementation of the Every Child Matters agenda.

The challenges for TAC practitioners

The challenges facing TAC members can be readily resolved by effective pre-planning, management and ongoing appropriate professional development for TAC practitioners. The main challenges faced by TAC practitioners are:

- **Time constraints** – The TAC can add to the workload of already busy practitioners, who may need to negotiate release time from some existing tasks, in order to carry out their TAC roles effectively, for example, SENCOs with full teaching commitments, and engaged in the TAC.

- **Training** – inter-professional training and development opportunities in how to work in multi-agency/multidisciplinary collaborative partnerships, as well as training in relationship building, is crucial but is not always a key focus of professional development.

- **Different service criteria and thresholds** – when the TAC lead professional considers a child's ability to achieve good ECM outcomes is, in their opinion, being hampered by the child's impoverished home background, but the social services threshold and criteria does not identify the same child and their family to be taken on as one of their cases, can result in frustration.

- **Tensions in relationships between parents and practitioners** – parents may feel let down by the TAC lead professional, who they trusted and considered to be on their side, when they are informed that they meet the social services thresholds/criteria for intervention and support, and they thought otherwise. It becomes crucial for the lead professional in such a situation to be debriefed by their line manager or another senior professional in their service.

Team Around the Child: lead professional, Common Assessment Framework and information sharing

The practitioners and professionals in the TAC will nominate and appoint a lead professional who will be responsible for ensuring that all agencies provide the agreed services to meet the identified needs of the child, young person and family, which were identified during the CAF process. The lead professional is most likely to be working in education, health or social care, and may be for example an educational welfare officer (EWO), a senior teacher, SENCO, learning mentor, school nurse, health visitor, youth worker, social worker, or a CAMHS worker. The lead professional acts as a single point of contact for the child, young person or family. They co-ordinate the delivery of agreed actions; they help to reduce any overlap or inconsistencies in service provision, and they take a lead role in ensuring intended outcomes are achieved by the team.

The essential qualities of a lead professional

The following list outlines the essential qualities parents and children value in a TAC lead professional:

- being an advocate for parents and children

- facilitating access to the right services at the right time

- being there for parents/carers when they need help

- being a good listener

- being positive

- using their initiative

- chairing meetings well

- knowledgeable and experienced in their own professional field

- knowledgeable about children and young people's needs.

The CAF and the lead professional cement the universal and preventative services around a child in a local area. The implementation and adoption of the CAF system is essential for the operational efficiency of the Team Around the Child.

Practitioners contributing to the CAF need to be able to synthesize and analyse the information and data gathered, and write up the information and outcomes in a comprehensive, jargon-free, parent-friendly format.

Information sharing and the Team Around the Child

The Data Protection Act 1998 provides a framework to help multi-agency practitioners share information lawfully and professionally. It is good practice to have a summary of the laws affecting information sharing in respect of children and young people available, as a point of reference for those multi-agency practitioners working in the educational setting.

Under the Data Protection Act 1998 certain information is exempt from disclosure and should be shared with other service providers. This includes:

- material whose disclosure would be likely to cause serious harm to the physical or mental health or emotional condition of the pupils or someone else

- information about whether the child is or has been subjected to or may be at risk of suspected child abuse

- references about pupils supplied to potential employers, to student admissions bodies, another school, a higher education/further education institution, or any other place of education or training

- information that may form part of a court report.

The government has also provided useful guidance for practitioners on information sharing, and they offer six key points:

1. Explain openly and honestly at the outset what information will or could be shared and why, and seek agreement and consent – except where doing so puts the child or others at risk of significant harm.

2. The child's safety and welfare must be the overriding consideration when making decisions on whether to share information about them.

3. Respect the wishes of children or families who do not consent to share confidential information – unless in your judgement there is sufficient need to override that lack of consent.

4. Seek advice when in doubt.

5. Ensure information is accurate, up-to-date, and necessary for the purpose for which you are sharing it, shared only with those who need to see it, and shared securely.

6. Always record the reasons for the decision – whether it is to share the information or not (DfES, 2006: 3).

Basic principles for information sharing

Any information should be:

- held securely

- obtained fairly and effectively

- recorded accurately and reliably

- used effectively and ethically

- shared appropriately and lawfully.

Multi-agency practitioners need also to check:

- that there is a legitimate purpose for them sharing the information

- whether the information enables a person/individual to be identified

- whether the information is confidential and, if it is, whether consent has been given to share the information

- whether there is a statutory duty or a court order to share the information

- that, if consent is refused or there are good reasons not to seek consent, there is sufficient public interest to share information

- whether individuals/services are sharing the right information in the right way

- that decisions arising from information sharing are properly recorded.

The National Service Framework and information sharing

The National Service Framework (NSF) for children, young people and maternity services also helps to establish good practice in information sharing between agencies. The NSF is an essential point of reference to those taking responsibility for overseeing and managing multi-agency partnership working within an educational setting. The NSF expects information to be:

- shared within the NHS and with and between other agencies

- helpful in identifying children and young people with additional needs

- kept up to date

- accessible knowledge which helps to improve care

- supporting early intervention to address the additional needs of children and young people

- improving the analysis and interpretation of data in order to better inform the direct care of children and young people

- informing the commissioning, managing and planning of multi-agency services

- made available to children, young people and their parents/carers in order to enable them to know the nature and impact of the services provided

- shared more efficiently and effectively through the use of information technology.

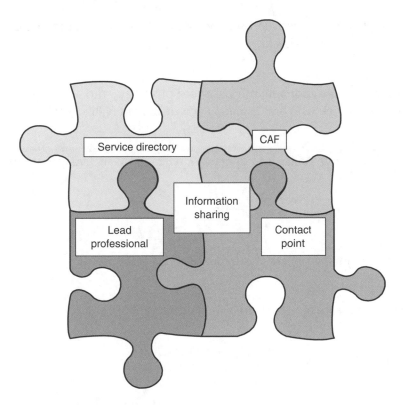

Figure 4.3   Integrated working in TAC

Small scale research into the Team Around the Child

Telford and Wrekin Council in partnership with Shropshire County Council com-missioned Jocelyn Jones of Mindful Practice Limited in 2006, to seek the views of children and young people, their families and those of TAC workers about the Team Around the Child.

The key messages from the research findings were as follows.

1. TAC workers need to take time to build the relationship and explain the TAC process with parents/carers, families and the child/young person, before the first TAC meeting.

2. Only to have the people who really need to be there at each TAC meeting.

Figure 4.4 Checklist for confidentiality and information sharing

☐ Information sharing that respects confidentiality is a key principle, providing the welfare and safety of the child or young person is not 'at risk' or likely to be compromised.

☐ Each service provider, the educational setting or children's centre makes explicit their policy and requirements regarding confidentiality.

☐ The Data Protection Act, information sharing protocols and procedures are clear to all partners and are correctly followed.

☐ Any highly case sensitive information is password protected, and can only be accessed by authorized personnel, who are Criminal Records Bureau (CRB) checked.

☐ An initial 'Need to Know' policy is in operation, which answers five key questions:

- What essential information is required?

- Under what circumstances can this information be released?

- To whom is it appropriate to release the information?

- How will the information be used?

- Will the released information be crucial to improving outcomes for the child or young person?

☐ It is made explicit when written consent is required for the release of information.

☐ All confidential conversations about children and families take place in a private sound-proofed office.

☐ All staff know about the information-sharing index: its purpose, information held and who can access information.

 Photocopiable:
Effective Multi-Agency Partnerships, Sage Publications © Rita Cheminais, 2009

3. Where and when the meetings are held and how long they go on for need to be agreed and then agreed again as things change. Short meetings of between one hour and one hour thirty minutes were preferred, with meetings being held outside school, where necessary.

4. If a worker cannot come to the meeting s/he should send their apologies in advance to parents/carers, the child/young person as well as to other TAC workers.

5. Talk in simple language at the meeting and make meetings as relaxed and friendly as possible.

6. You (*children/young people*) appreciated seeing results from the TAC plans like, '*This is what we've got for you*'.

7. Negotiate time to debrief the child/young person and/or parents and carers, following a TAC meeting, which could be done by the lead professional.

8. Being listened to is REALLY important. Counselling, building on good behaviour, and the occasional 'wake-up call' also helped.

9. Year 8 and Year 9 were when parents indicated their child needed earlier help and intervention for non-attendance at school or for behaviour problems.

10. Sometimes it might be better to have a TAC meeting without a parent(s) being there.

11. The role of the lead professional is crucial to building good relationships, but they need administrative support during TAC meetings, in order to enable them to chair meetings effectively.

12. Choice about how to take part in future evaluations matters, and needs to be agreed with each child/young person. (Jones, 2006: 2–3)

✝✝✝✝ Team Around the Child development task

In the context of the educational setting you are currently working in as a member of a TAC, compare your findings after using the survey in Figure 4.5, with

---

Team Around the Child Survey

Please ✓ TAC worker   Parent/carer   Child/young person   Other (please state)

1. How do you think the Team Around the Child (TAC) has helped to make a real difference?

2. What do you think about the TAC process?

3. What three key messages do you have to give to the TAC workers?

4. What did you like the best about the TAC?

5. What did you like the least about the TAC?

6. How could the TAC be improved in the future?

7. Is there anything further you wish to comment on about the TAC?

Figure 4.5   Team Around the Child survey

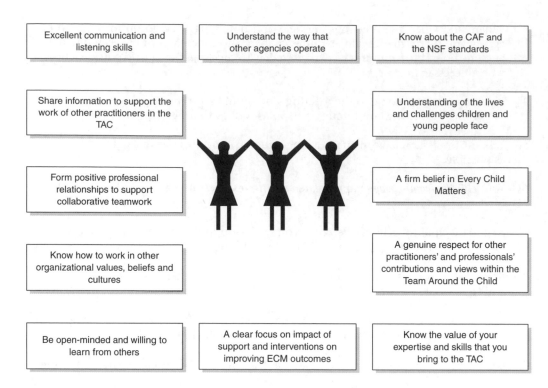

Figure 4.6   The essential skills and knowledge required by practitioners in the Team Around the Child

those of Jocelyn Jones. Share and discuss your findings with key stakeholders, and use the evidence to inform future improvements and developments in TAC partnership working.

Key elements of good practice in Team Around the Child

Peter Limbrick identified the following elements of good practice in Team Around the Child working.

- Each child's key practitioners agree to work as a closely collaborative and individualized team who are collectively responsive to the needs of the child.

- Parents are equal members and partners of the TAC, and they have a 'voice'.

- A key worker or lead professional facilitates each individual team. The child's development and learning programmes are integrated as far as possible, as part of a coherent holistic approach.

- There is a proactive effort to ensure that each TAC is founded in effective relationships (Limbrick, 2005: 6).

✝✝✝✝ Individual TAC team member reflection task

- Identify the factors that have enabled you as a TAC practitioner to approach a problem in a new way.

- What have you learned from this TAC collaborative partnership working experience?

- What else do you feel you can contribute to the team around the child?

- What do you need to do to further improve your team-working skills?

- When do you find it most difficult to work in the team around the child?

- When do you most enjoy team-working in the team around the child?

- What do you do when you are faced with a difficult issue that has arisen from the team around the child partnership working situation?

Points to remember

- The Team Around the Child (TAC) adopt a needs-led approach to improving ECM outcomes for children/young people.
- The lead professional in the TAC co-ordinates provision and ensures that all agencies provide services to meet a child's needs.
- The Common Assessment Framework is essential to the efficient operation of the Team Around the Child.
- Parents/carers of the child are equal partners within the TAC.
- Parents/carers and their child, need to know what the TAC process is all about, prior to their involvement and its commencement.

Further activities

The following reflective questions, based on aspects covered in this chapter are designed to enable members of the Team Around the Child, working in the educational setting, to identify aspects of their working practice that requires further development and improvement.

- How do you intend to explain the aims, purpose and process of the Team Around the Child to parents/carers and their children?

- What is it like being a member of this Team Around the Child?

- What worked best in the Team Around the Child?

- What did not work well in the Team Around the Child?

- What frustrates you about the Team Around the Child?

Figure 4.7 Exemplar Team Around the Child information leaflet for parents and children

INFORMATION LEAFLET

INSERT YOUR
SCHOOL BADGE OR
SETTING LOGO HERE

TEAM AROUND THE CHILD

IN

(INSERT YOUR SCHOOL'S/SETTING'S NAME HERE)

Introduction

This leaflet explains what the Team Around the Child is, and how it helps children and their families in Maple School.

What is the Team Around the Child?

The Team Around the Child brings together workers from different services such as education, health and social care to form a small team of between three to six people, who provide regular help and practical support to a child and their family, when needed.

Sometimes the Team Around the Child may have staff from the school on it, such as the SEN Co-ordinator, a Learning Mentor, or an Assistant Headteacher.

Every Team Around the Child has a lead professional in it who checks that all the different agencies involved provide the agreed services to meet the needs of the child and their family.

Parents/carers and their child can get in touch with the lead professional at any time, and they will listen to any concerns.

(Continued)

Figure 4.7 (Continued)

What does the Team Around the Child do?

The Team Around the Child delivers joined-up well-co-ordinated services to help to improve a child's learning, behaviour, health and well-being.

The Team around the Child reviews the support being given to the child and family, and reports on the progress being made.

Parents and carers and their child's involvement in the Team Around the Child is valued and seen as being important.

What happens at Team Around the Child meetings?

The Team Around the Child workers meet with the parents and carers and the child, where appropriate, for one hour, either in school, or out of school, at an agreed place. The meetings are relaxed and friendly, and everything that is discussed is easy to understand.

Parents and carers are equal partners in the Team Around the Child, and their views about the progress their child has made are listened to in the meeting.

Every service worker in the team reports back on how their support has helped the child to improve.

Following the meeting, at an agreed time, parents and carers and their child can obtain further information or explanation from the lead professional about agreed outcomes and next steps.

What are the benefits of the Team Around the Child?

- A small team of multi-agency workers really get to know the child and their family well.
- Services are more easily accessible locally, within, or near the school site.
- Everyone in the Team Around the Child is working closely together to ensure that all the child's needs are met.
- Good relationships of trust are built up between the Team Around the Child workers, the family and the child.
- The lead professional is a regular point of contact for the child and their family.
- Only one common assessment takes place to identify the child and family's needs.

Further information

If you want to find out more information about the Team Around the Child, then visit the following websites.

www.mapletac.sch.uk

www.everychildmatters.gov.uk

You can also visit the OASIS Centre in the school for further information, or make an appointment to meet with the school's Every Child Matters Co-ordinator.

- What issues, concerns or problems have arisen in the Team Around the Child, and how have these come about?

- What could other members of the TAC do to support you in resolving such issues, problems or concerns?

- What would you change or do differently next time in order to improve the effectiveness of the Team Around the Child?

Further information

The following websites have downloadable resources that can help to support the development and work of the Team Around the Child, within the educational setting.

www.everychildmatters.gov.uk   This website has information about the Team Around the Child and multi-agency working.

www.icwhatsnew.com   This website provides a selection of Peter Limbrick's documents and other resources related to the principles and practice of Team Around the Child and multi-agency service co-ordination.

www.mindfulpractice.co.uk   This website contains the executive summary report of the evaluation of the Team Around the Child Trailblazer project. It also provides links to Peter Limbrick's key documents on the Team Around the Child.

www.shropshire.gov.uk/isa.nsf/open/D4C5EF6293436CC48025725F0050EA43   This website provides a comprehensive range of material about the practicalities of the operation of the Team Around the Child. It has exemplars of good practice regarding TAC meetings, and it also provides useful website links to further information about the Team Around the Child.

www.dataprotection.gov.uk   This website provides further detailed information about data protection and offers helpful guidelines for services and agencies.

www.everychildmatters.gov.uk   This website has further information and a helpful checklist in relation to information-sharing protocols in the DfES document *Inter-Agency Information Sharing Criteria*. There are two other useful documents available on this website called *A Framework for Information Sharing* and *A Step-by-Step Guide to Writing Information Sharing Protocols*.

Do not forget to also visit the Sage website (www.sagepub.co.uk/cheminais) for downloadable resources to use with this chapter.

5

The Features of Good Practice in Multi-Agency Partnership Working

> **This chapter describes:**
>
> - **The features that are key to the successful implementation of ECM**
> - **The key features of good practice in multi-agency partnership working**
> - **The essential qualities for making a good multi-agency partner**
> - **Cameos of effective multi-agency partnership working**
> - **Practical activities for reflecting on collaborative partnership working**

This chapter is useful to those researching good practice in multi-agency working.

The features that lead to the successful implementation of ECM

Collaborative working is at the heart of the Every Child Matters agenda. Every Child Matters has facilitated a common approach among multi-agency practitioners, by enabling them to share concerns and work more closely together. Leaders in educational settings recognize that they cannot deliver the ECM outcomes in isolation, and that different agencies and services have different expertise to contribute. School leaders in particular, acknowledge that they must be open-minded, engage in regular dialogue with those from agencies and services about what they both want out of the partnership, develop mutual trust and become familiar with the various multi-agency professional frames of reference.

The key features in schools, where ECM is successfully being implemented include the following strengths and characteristics, according to Harris:

- ECM is the central priority that drives the school's developmental agenda

- Leadership is aspirational and is commonly focused

- Local authority support and guidance is of the highest standard

- Funding is used strategically and creatively to support the core priorities and the ECM agenda

- Leadership is distributed in the optimum way for the school and its partners

- Parents, governors and community groups are involved in decision-making

- Targeted training is provided to staff, pupils, and the community

- ECM is aligned to workforce remodelling

- The school has a strong internal locus of control; it is innovative, confident and outward looking

- ECM and the extended school initiative are considered to be central to raising standards

- ECM and the extended school initiative are acknowledged as a pupil and community entitlement. (Harris et al., 2007: 70–1)

The key features of good practice in successful multi-agency partnership working

Atkinson, et al., (2007) identified the essential key factors to successful multi-agency good practice as being:

- commitment from those involved at all levels

- good working relationships based on trust and mutual respect

- regular professional meetings for planning

- good leadership

- joint funding, which ideally leads to equal resource distribution

- having common joint aims and objectives

- having the relevant professionals involved who can give continuity

- having a clear focus for the work

- having joint ownership.

Tomlinson in 2003, identified other features of good practice for successful multi-agency working:

- full strategic and operational commitment to collaboration

- awareness of differing aims and values whilst working towards a common goal

- involvement of all relevant parties, including children/young people, and parents/carers

- clear roles and responsibilities for individuals and agencies involved, ensuring parity among all partners

- flexible and innovative mechanisms

- supportive and committed management of staff

- systems for collecting, sharing and analysing data

- joint training to foster greater understanding between agencies

- strategies to support team commitment

- effective and appropriate communication

- a suitable location for delivery

- sufficient time for the development of multi-agency working.

✝✝✝✝ Task 5.1: Group practical task – multi-agency working: good practice outcomes

- Read the ten statements below about the outcomes resulting from multi-agency integrated working.

- Discuss the statements with other members in your group.

- Reach a consensus in your group about which **one** statement you are going to discard.

- Rank the remaining nine statements in order of priority.

- Read the statements again, looking for similarities and differences.

- Select **five** of the statements that all the group agree are the most important, and arrange in order of priority.

1. Every Child Matters outcomes improve for children/young people.

2. More effective ways of working occur.

3. The educational setting/children's centre gets a good reputation locally for its multi-agency working.

4. Practitioners from different services can think creatively and be innovative.

Table 5.1   Summary of effective multi-agency practice strategies

Effective multi-agency practice strategies	
Working relationships	
Clarifying roles and responsibilities	• Take time initially to clarify roles and responsibilities of all parties • Each worker should have a clear role and sense of contribution • Recognize and value differences, value diversity • Joint training can help to clarify roles, and shared learning in groups can reduce stereotypes • Provide time to allow professionals to reflect on their new professional identities • Reduce 'turf issues' by pre-planning and highlighting the positive outcomes of collaboration and disseminating those from other service collaborations • Ensure parity in the perceived seniority of representatives from different organizations • Foster respect for specialist expertise combined with a willingness to explore and celebrate professional diversity • Boundary crossing can lead to a renegotiation of professional practice
Securing commitment at all levels	• Multi-agency work requires commitment at both strategic and operational levels • Foster personal commitment rather than professionals being directed to work in a multi-agency way • Ensure that the professional involved can see the benefits of multi-agency work as this secures greater commitment and stops it from floundering • Provide opportunities for sharing goals and visions, establishing trust and mutual responsibility as this helps secure commitment • Creating opportunities for decision-making and effectively chairing meetings encourage attendance • Ensure that part-time, peripheral or seconded staff feel included • Consult with professionals and clients from the beginning to secure commitment • A strong history of collaboration raises levels of commitment • Commitment should be underpinned by resources • Leadership modelling commitment heightens commitment levels
Engendering trust and mutual respect	• Development of close working relationships aids honesty and encourages open discussions of problems • Sharing skills and expertise develops trust, as does a willingness to be honest regarding knowledge gaps • Shared visions and equal resource distribution develop trust
Fostering understanding between agencies	• Joint training and forums can help to foster understanding between agencies • Recognition of the unique roles of individuals and utilization of all skills • Work shadowing schemes can enhance understanding • Key players should be given time together to foster mutual understanding and informed dialogue

Table 5.1   (Continued)

Effective multi-agency practice strategies

	• Accessible, practical guides to working with different sectors
	• Appointing a leader with 'cultural intelligence' who can identify the different cultures and construct an appropriate response
	• Provide opportunities to cross-boundaries, to examine current practice for each agency and to rethink the multi-agency philosophy
	• Give the culture of partnership and collaboration high priority
	• Basing strategic level staff in a reluctant department can raise the profile of multi-agency working
	• Take time to learn and understand each agency's mission, priorities and technical language
	• Staff secondments into partner agencies or presentations from different agencies at the start of collaboration can help to break down barriers
Multi-agency processes	
Ensuring effective communication and information sharing	• Create transparent lines of communication with clear protocols
	• Increased contact through meetings, working groups or training etc., results in greater inclination to seek further communication
	• Create frequent opportunities for communication, discussion and debate
	• Face-to-face meetings and a mix of formal and informal modes of communication
	• Develop personal connections to promote working relationships and informal links
	• Co-location of services where possible
	• Provide accessible, written updates, particularly at early stages of multi-agency partnerships
	• Have a proactive approach to communication and embed into working practices
	• Formalize processes for information sharing and establish clear protocols
	• Provide joint training to facilitate information sharing and the exchange of good practice
	• Ensure that all representatives understand all terms or acronyms and provide definitions of the most common terms
	• Explore any differences in terminology as a group and consider any different understandings
	• Key players in multi-agency groups might benefit from more time together to foster informed dialogue
	• Team activities and service development should allow for creation of a shared language
Developing a shared purpose	• Develop a shared vision to define the scope and purpose of the partnership and use this as a reference point
	• The shared vision should be inspirational and based on jointly held values

(Continued)

Table 5.1   (Continued)

Effective multi-agency practice strategies	
	• Develop a shared understanding
	• Have a clear justification for partnership and demonstrate value for money
	• Develop clarity of roles and responsibilities (role demarcation)
	• Ensure targets and objectives are relevant and shared across agencies
	• Clearly articulate goals and outcomes
	• Develop guidelines to show how services are co-ordinated
	• Provide joint training or staff development
	• Set up a steering group to identify problems, key issues and different cultures
	• Conduct a needs analysis to create a picture of existing provision and boundaries of provision
Effective planning and organization	• Consult service users on needs, issues and priorities in a way that empowers them and is sustainable
	• Use well designed consultations, good instruments and strategies etc.
	• Develop shared protocols and written commitment to inter-professional working that are reviewed regularly
	• Develop a clearly defined and well documented structure/model to explain multi-agency operation and make this available to service users
	• Set up systems and structures to support joint working, such as service level agreements, co-ordinating bodies and multi-professional groups
	• Understand and cater for distinctive working conditions and the aims and objectives of different sectors
	• Disseminate good practice
	• Provide joint training to develop common ways of working
	• Use task groups to transform strategic plans into operational action
	• Adopt pro-collaboration policies and inform front-line staff
	• Select representation purposefully, ensuring equal representation
	• Balance the need to involve all organizations with the need to deliver partnership objectives efficiently and involve all relevant agencies early
	• Use a checklist of all agencies involved with the client group
	• Ensure representation of service users where relevant
	• Deliver any new functions through existing partnerships wherever possible
	• Assess the variability of members' history of collaboration when bringing a multi-agency group together
	• Provide training to those inexperienced in multi-agency work
	• Where there are few inherited linkages, proactive networking at strategic levels could counterbalance this

Table 5.1   (Continued)

Effective multi-agency practice strategies

Resources for multi-agency work

Securing adequate and sustained funding	• Pooled budgets or joint funding
	• Identify and use alternative sources of funding
	• Avoid asking individuals to be involved in multi-agency work without additional funding, i.e. while still being held accountable for their full workload
	• Ensure stability of funding and distribute resources equally across agencies
	• Produce and agree clearly written agreements for funding arrangements
	• Recognition by senior managers of the importance of shared resources and the need to act as champions for funding arrangements at strategic/operational levels
	• Ensure dedicated resources to keep everyone engaged
	• Resources should be available to support management and administration
Ensuring continuity of staffing	• Support leaders and delegate responsibility to alleviate problems with staff turnover
	• Consider capacity issues to ensure continuity of representation over time
	• Facilitation through co-location, a joint location or a change in location
Ensuring adequate time	• Build in time for planning, developing and implementing arrangements
	• Sufficient groundwork on team building and developing trust
	• Create time for reflecting on new professional identities
	• Have a project start up phase for planning and development

Management and governance

Ensuring effective leadership	• Senior positions have more clout than junior staff in management roles
	• Leaders require shared vision and tenacity to drive the agenda as well as full commitment, strong entrepreneurial skills and net-working
	• Partnerships need sustained input from leadership and leaders need time and resources for their role
	• Reorganize work to ensure that managers can get time to get involved
	• Leaders should consult with and provide support for front-line staff, as well as addressing service conditions and staff welfare
	• Provide support networks for leaders and some delegation of other staff to relieve pressures
	• Leaders should model commitment to maximize collaboration
Establishing appropriate governance systems	• Processes/structures of accountability need to be appropriate to the type of partnership and make sense to front-line workers

(Continued)

Table 5.1   (Continued)

Effective multi-agency practice strategies

	• Have clear roles and responsibility for the accountable body
	• Give accountability to external stakeholders and be accountable to service users
	• Consistency of governance structures with the vision and approach the partnership is taking, and facilitate efficient and effective decision-making
Establishing performance management systems	• Clear aims and objectives and joint performance indicators
	• Performance management systems that reflect the complexity of partnership working, capture a range of activity and have a clear focus on outcomes
	• Have joint review and evaluation procedures (e.g. team away days)

Source: Atkinson et al., 2007: 80–4 reproduced with permission from NFER and CfBT (2007)

5. Positive change is acknowledged, celebrated and publicized.

6. Multi-agency team working leads to greater job satisfaction.

7. A way of doing something is improved.

8. Clients experience greater satisfaction as a result of receiving the multi-agency integrated services support and intervention.

9. Cross-agency tensions and conflicts are reduced.

10. Joint ownership and responsibility for decision-making occurs.

The essential qualities for making a good multi-agency partner

According to Smarter Partnerships, a good multi-agency partner is someone who:

• wants the partnership to succeed

• seeks win-win solutions

• is open and clear about their own goals

• listens well and responds to other views

• is prepared to trust

• has integrity and acts consistently

- effectively carries out their tasks and responsibilities

- respects others and their contributions

- is not prepared to sweep difficulties under the carpet

- can be flexible but retains focus

- understands how partners depend on one another

- leads their colleagues in support of collaboration (www.lgpartnerships.com/resources/ trust-whatmakes.asp).

Examples of good practice in multi-agency working

The following exemplars of good practice in multi-agency working with educational settings, are aligned to the Every Child Matters (ECM) outcomes. The blank templates (Table 5.2a and 5.2b), offer two models to enable educational settings and children's centres to gather their evidence of the impact of multi-agency partnership working succinctly, to feed into the OFSTED self-evaluation form (SEF).

The examples in this chapter are taken from government research into BEST (DfES, 2005); from the Integrated Working Exemplars (DCSF, 2007a, 2007b, 2007c), on the government's Every Child Matters website, and from local authority children's services, for example, Cambridgeshire County Council (2006). The good practice exemplars of multi-agency working in children's centres are taken from the CWDC/TFC (2007) document which featured cameos of practice in the East of England. While there are many more examples of good practice in multi-agency working with schools and children's centres in existence, the selected exemplars are designed to act as a model of how an educational setting or a children's centre can organize their own examples under each of the five ECM outcomes.

Table 5.2a Template for sharing good practice in multi-agency working

Name of the organization	
Multi-agency activity	
Target group	
Aims of the activity	
Expected outcomes	
Actual outcomes	
ECM outcome(s) met	
Brief description of the activity (What did you do? How did you do it?)	
Other agencies and services involved	
Resources needed	
Cost of activity (Money and time)	
What would you change or do differently next time?	

Source: Author's own

 Photocopiable:
Effective Multi-Agency Partnerships, Sage Publications © Rita Cheminais, 2009

Table 5.2b Multi-agency good practice template

THE APPROACH **What is the overall aim of the project/multi-agency work?**
How does the project/work link with the Every Child Matters outcomes?
How was the multi-agency work undertaken in practice?
What were/are the main challenges?
IN PRACTICE **Potential/actual impact of the work/project?**
What were the outcomes of the multi-agency work/project?
CONCLUSIONS
NEXT STEPS **Do you intend to continue and/or develop this work further?**
Can you summarize how this piece of multi-agency work may assist other children's centres/extended schools?

Source: adapted from Together for Children (TFC) case study framework proforma VI (2007)

 Photocopiable:

Effective Multi-Agency Partnerships, Sage Publications © Rita Cheminais, 2009

Table 5.3   Exemplar of multi-agency working – ECM outcome: Be healthy

Name of lead service:	Health – CAMHS
Multi-agency activity:	Assessment, intervention and support to meet the mental health needs of children and young people with learning difficulties
Target group:	Children and young people with a learning disability and a mental health problem
Aims of the activity:	Early intervention meets needs; assessment, treatment, consultation provided promptly; liaison with the family, the educational setting/children's centre, and other services and agencies; appropriate programme of support put in place; provide a mental health link worker for the setting; provide training to staff in the setting
Brief description of the activity:	An assessment of the child's mental health needs is undertaken at home, school or at the local clinic. From the results of the assessment an appropriate programme of support is put in place to meet the needs.
	A social care outreach worker provides support and counselling to the child and their family
Other agencies/services involved:	Social Care SEN and Disability Team
Outcomes/impact:	• The child/young person and their family have attended all appointments and sessions • The child/young person is better able to manage • Other professionals/practitioners have a better understanding of the child/young person's mental health problems • The child/young person and their family feel well supported

Source: adapted from Cambridgeshire County Council, 2006: 6

Table 5.4   Exemplar of multi-agency working – ECM outcome: Be healthy

Name of lead service:	Education – Learning Mentor
Multi-agency activity:	Provide advice, support and direct interventions to improve the behaviour and social skills of the child
Target group:	A 7-year-old girl who is becoming disobedient in class, aggressive towards other children, and difficult to manage at home
Aims of the activity:	Improve the child's behaviour
	Enable the child to understand the feelings of others
	Enable the child to participate in co-operative play
	To develop the child's social skills

Table 5.4   (Continued)

Brief description of the activity:	School nurse gives parents advice about how to stop the child bed-wetting
	Playground assistants provide structured play activities
	After-school Bubble club provides activities on: making friends, taking turns, thinking about feelings
	'Bears' and BEST teams provide interventions to improve the child's behaviour
	BEST provide class teacher with classroom behaviour management strategies
Other agencies/services involved:	School nurse
	BEST
	'Bears' multi-agency team – part of CAMHS
Outcomes/impact:	• Child's behaviour improves at home
	• Child is no longer disruptive in class
	• Parents can now manage their child's behaviour
	• Child enjoys participating in extended school activities
	• Child has better relationships with parents
	• Child has a supportive circle of friends at school

Source: adapted from DCSF, 2007a © Crown copyright 2007

Table 5.5   Children's centre exemplar of multi-agency working – ECM outcome: Be healthy

Name of lead service:	Health service: Southampton Primary Care Trust
Multi-agency activity:	Data and information sharing on progress made in relation to: low birth weight rates, normal delivery rates, smoking rates of mothers, breastfeeding rates, obesity rates among children in Reception year
Target group:	Children under the age of 5, and mothers of pre-school children in children's centres
Aims of the activity:	To find ways of sharing appropriate data collected by Southampton City Primary Care Trust and Southampton University Hospitals Trust with Sure Start children's centres and their stakeholders to track progress, and stimulate debate about improving outcomes
Brief description of the activity:	Identification of what information is already collected and developing agreements for sharing information.
	Making the data collection system more robust.
	Presenting data on outcomes in a more user-friendly format for parents and practitioners
Other agencies/services involved:	Education – Heads of children's centres

(Continued)

Table 5.5   (Continued)

Outcomes/impact:	• Better information sharing • Improved parental and local practitioner involvement and ownership of targets • Improved health for some of the city's most vulnerable children • Enabled comparisons to be made between children's centres in the area to help identify good practice, and inform resource allocation

Source: TFC, 2007

Table 5.6   Children's centre exemplar of multi-agency working – ECM outcomes: Be healthy and Enjoy and achieve

Name of lead service:	Health – PCT: Speech and Language therapy service London Borough of Barking and Dagenham
Multi-agency activity:	Develop a joint model of service delivery by working in partnership with Children's Services and the PCT to deliver effective speech and language services
Target group:	Pre-school aged children under 5 in all the children's centres
Aims of the activity:	Provide a preventative speech and language service through all 14 children's centres
	Increase the percentage of children who achieve a total of at least 78 points across the FSP with at least 6 points scored in each of the PESD and CLL scales
Brief description of the activity:	Early identification and screening of children at risk of developing communication delay/disorder and learning difficulties
	Early intervention for those children identified with language and communication delay or disorder
	Targeted support services for children and their families, which include advice, guidance and training, and include infant massage, Babbling Babes, Toddler Talk, Little Rhyme Makers, messy food play, parent play and communication workshops, speech and language drop-ins, home visits and outreach
	Working with parents/carers and others agencies to ensure a holistic approach to developing a child's CLL and PSED well before they start school
Other agencies/ services involved:	Health visitors Community nursery nurses Play and communication workers in children's centres Family support team Portage team
Outcomes/impact:	• Decrease in the number of referrals to SALT service • Enhanced early parent-infant interaction and parent/carer's skills in

Table 5.6   (Continued)

	supporting their child's development of speech, language and communication.
	• Increased skills of early years staff in identifying and supporting children's speech, language and communication.
	• Established integrated working arrangements with other agencies

Source: TFC, 2007

Table 5.7   Exemplar of multi-agency working – ECM outcome: Stay safe

Name of lead service:	BEST
Multi-agency activity:	Production of a leaflet on *How to Have a Party Safely* for teenagers in the local area.
Target group:	Children and young people aged 11–18
Aim of the activity:	to make teenagers aware of the dangers of substance misuse, alcohol in excess, and unprotected sex
Brief description of the activity:	Children/young people are supported by BEST to research the production of a leaflet for pupils in the school to help them stay safe at parties
	The school nurse delivers sessions as part of the school's PSHE programme on alcohol and drug misuse as well as safe sexual relationships
Other agencies/ services involved:	Health – school nurse
Outcomes/impact:	• getting the message across to teenagers about safety at parties
	• involvement of teenagers in the production of the leaflet gives greater credibility
	• fewer reported incidents in the local community of antisocial behaviour or ill health as a result of alcohol, substance misuse
	• a reduction in the number of teenage pregnancies in the local area

Source: adapted from Cambridgeshire County Council 2006: 7

Table 5.8   Exemplar of multi-agency working – ECM outcomes: Stay safe and Enjoy and achieve

Name of lead service:	Education – Learning Mentor
Multi-agency activity:	Multi-agency provision to enable a disaffected boy to enjoy learning more, and be happier at home
Target group:	A bright 13-year-old dyslexic boy with truancy and transition issues, who is misbehaving in class, being excluded from sports lessons, is not finishing his homework, and has poor attendance. He is not happy at home and does not like his mother's new partner, and is still missing his dead father

(Continued)

Table 5.8 (Continued)

Aims of the activity:	Improve his attitude, behaviour and self-confidence. Improve his attendance at school and his motivation for school work Help him come to terms with his father's death Enable him to get on with his mother's new partner
Brief description of the activity:	Parent support adviser (PSA) and EWO work with the boy and his mother to improve his attendance. Learning Mentor and the boy meet weekly for a one-to-one to discuss any issues or concerns. TA is put in boy's class in English, History and Geography School nurse gives him bereavement counselling Connexions PA gets him access to youth service activities, and gives advice on options at 14. He benefits from the whole school SEAL initiative
Other agencies/services involved:	Parent support adviser (PSA) Education welfare officer (EWO) Connexions personal adviser School nurse Youth service
Outcomes/impact:	• Attendance improves at school • Better relationships at home with mum's partner • Not out at night as much, spending more time at home • Self-confidence of the boy has improved • The boy has come to terms with his father's death • The boy joins a peer mentoring scheme in school to help younger pupils

Source: adapted from DCSF, 2007b © Crown copyright 2007

Table 5.9 Exemplar of multi-agency working – ECM outcomes: Enjoy and achieve

Name of lead service:	Connexions
Multi-agency activity:	To provide an alternative personalized curriculum for a group of ten Year 10 lower-attaining pupils
Target group:	Disaffected cohort of Year 10 lower-attaining pupils
Aims of the activity:	To provide a more relevant motivating curriculum To improve the attendance of the cohort of pupils To provide pupils with important key skills
Brief description of the activity:	The initiative is led by the Connexions PA who has worked with the Director of Curriculum Studies in the school to produce a tailored, personalized and work-related programme for the target group of pupils. The motivating

Table 5.9   (Continued)

	programme entails one day a week in a work placement; one day at the local FE college and three days in school following their regular curriculum. The EWO monitors the pupils' attendance. The youth worker provides after-school activities for the pupils' to engage in. The learning mentor tracks and monitors pupils' progress. The counsellor provides one-to-one sessions to seek the pupils' views on the initiative and help to build their self-esteem
Other agencies/services involved:	Education welfare officer (EWO) Youth service Counsellor
Outcomes/impact:	• The attendance of all the Year 10 pupils improves • The attitude, self-esteem and behaviour of the pupils improves • The pupils basic skills and social skills improve

Table 5.10   Exemplar of multi-agency working – ECM outcomes: Be healthy, Stay safe and Enjoy and achieve

Name of lead service:	Children's Social Care
Multi-agency activity:	Wrap-around care to safeguard a vulnerable and abused teenager
Target group:	A troubled young male teenager aged 14 who has been found by the police in central London after a shop-lifting offence. His father is physically violent to his son and the boy's mother. Mother is not coping and the boy is not getting regular meals at home. The boy has poor attendance at school. He has not been doing his homework, and he has been rude and challenging to his teachers at school
Aims of the activity:	Ensure the boy is safe and away from his violent dad. Improve his attitude and motivation to learning. Enable the boy to enjoy his leisure and football. Improve his attendance at school Ensure the boy is more relaxed and happy at home
Brief description of the activity:	Police refer the boy to Children's Social Care Service. Social care worker takes the boy to A&E for X-ray. The boy has injuries from his father. Social care worker puts the boy

(Continued)

Table 5.10   (Continued)

	with foster carers and refers his mother to domestic violence unit, who accommodate her in local women's refuge and to the mental health service for her depression. The father is removed from the home by an exclusion order. He is imprisoned. The boy and his mother return to the family home. The Youth Service provide activities for the boy. Family Support Worker helps the boy to resettle at home with his mother, and he receives counselling. Connexions PA provides the boy with career advice
Other agencies/services involved:	Police, social care worker, family support worker, health service, CAMHS – therapist, youth service, Connexions, specialist voluntary organization
Outcomes/impact:	
	• The boy helps his mother more at home • The boy makes new friends • The boy enjoys football and out of school activities • The boy is keeping up with his coursework at school • The boy is happier and relaxed at home • The father is not allowed to contact his son or his wife.

Source: adapted from DCSF, 2007c © Crown copyright 2007

Table 5.11   Exemplar of multi-agency working – ECM outcomes: Make a positive contribution

Name of lead service:	Youth Service
Multi-agency activity:	To provide free wall space in a town to prevent the further spread of graffiti around the town centre
Target group:	Cohort of teenagers who are doing the unsightly graffiti across the town
Aims of the activity:	To reduce and eradicate the unsightly graffiti around the town
Brief description of the activity:	The Youth Service in partnership with the parish council meet with the teenagers doing the graffiti to agree to one wall being made available for artistic graffiti to be done by teenagers instead of around the town. The local Community Safety Partnership fund half the project and an adult graffiti artist is commissioned to work with the teenagers to produce artistic graffiti on the free wall
Other agencies/services involved:	Parish council Professional adult graffiti artist Community Safety Partnership
Outcomes/impact:	• Major drop in graffiti around the town • Teenagers take more responsibility to ensure that graffiti only takes place on the free wall • Teenagers are responsible for updating the graffiti display on the free wall

Source: adapted from Cambridgeshire County Council 2006: 15–16

Table 5.12   Children's centre exemplar of multi-agency working – ECM outcome: Make a positive contribution

Name of lead service:	Education – Early Years Advisory Team Hertfordshire
Multi-agency activity:	Young children's participation project
Target group:	Pre-school children aged under 5 in children's centres and early years settings
Aims of the activity:	To ensure that the voice of the under 5s is noted in the Hertfordshire Children's Charter
Brief description of the activity:	The project was rolled out to all children's centres and Early Years settings. Early years workers were given advice, guidance and training in how to engage the voice of the young child, and to ensure their views are valued and listened to by adults, as well as the importance of involving young children in participation and consultation
Other agencies/services involved:	Health – community nurses Family support workers
Outcomes/impact:	• A children's champion or voice in every children's centre and early years setting • Respectful adults who children can trust to not manipulate what they say • The voice of the child is embedded in everyday practice • Helped to implement the UN Charter for the Child

Source: CWDC/TFC, 2007: 9

Table 5.13   Exemplar of multi-agency working – ECM outcome: Achieve economic well-being

Name of lead service:	Housing department
Multi-agency activity:	To produce a guide for young people about how to avoid being homeless
Target group:	Young people at risk of being homeless
Aims of the activity:	Raise awareness about the risks of homelessness Provide information about the range of accommodation available in the local area, and who to contact
Brief description of the activity:	Social care, Connexions and the Housing Department have worked together to produce a user-friendly guide for young people about homelessness, and how to find safe, low cost accommodation locally
Other agencies/services involved:	Social care, Connexions
Outcomes/impact:	• Improved service provision for the young homeless • Reduced the number of young people who are homeless in the local area • Enabled those working with young people to feel confident and better informed about advising young people on finding suitable accommodation

Source: adapted from Cambridgeshire County Council, 2006: 18

Points to remember

- Use a common template to record consistently, all the multi-agency activities and their impact on improving outcomes for children.
- ECM must be the central priority that drives raising standards and improving children and young people's well-being, in relation to multi-agency working.
- Having a clear focus for multi-agency work within the setting, is crucial.
- There needs to be a strategic and operational commitment to collaborative partnership working existing within the setting.

Further activities

The following activities, based on information in this chapter, are designed to help managers and front-line practitioners identify the good practice features of multi-agency partnership working.

- What does good practice in multi-agency working look like in your educational setting/ children's centre?

- Think of **one** successful ECM multi-agency partnership activity you have either led or been involved in. Briefly describe this activity.

- What was the aim of this selected multi-agency activity?

- Indicate what the impact of the multi-agency activity had on improving the ECM outcomes for the target group of children/young people.

- Who will you talk to in the next couple of weeks about what you have learned about multi-agency partnership working in your setting?

- Why will you talk to that particular person, about your multi-agency partnership working experiences?

- What has been the best bit of professional learning for you in relation to multi-agency working?

- What resources, books and websites have you found to be useful in relation to helping you to understand and improve your own multi-agency partnership working?

- What are the features of good practice in multi-agency communication in your own setting?

- What evidence can be found of other emerging good practice in multi-agency innovative work in your local area?

- How has good practice in multi-agency working been identified and disseminated?

Further information

The following websites have downloadable exemplars of good practice in multi-agency working.

www.ecm.gov.uk/integratedworking/exemplars   There are five exemplars of a child or young person who is vulnerable and experiencing difficulties at home and in school. Each example takes you on the ideal journey through accessing a range of multi-agency services to improve out-comes. The exemplars link to the NSF and ECM outcomes frameworks.

www.childrens-centres.org/default.aspx   This website has case studies/cameos of integrated working in children's centres in the East of England, as well as other information about children's centres.

Do not forget to also visit the Sage website (www.sagepub.co.uk/cheminais) for downloadable resources to use with this chapter.

Evaluating the Impact and Outcomes of Multi-Agency Partnership Working

---

This chapter exemplifies:

- **The range of tools available for evaluating the impact and outcomes of multi-agency provision**
- **How to evaluate the impact of multi-agency partnership working**
- **Surveying the views of service providers and service users**
- **Key questions for exploring the next steps for further improving multi-agency partnership working**

This chapter is useful for leaders in education settings/children's centres.

When evaluating the impact of multi-agency provision it must be remembered that this is only one part of the sum of the whole continuum of provision for improving Every Child Matters outcomes for children and young people in an educational setting. This factor accounts for why the exact impact of ECM upon the achievements of children and young people is difficult to disaggregate. A behaviour support teacher remarked:

> Some of these children are so damaged that you're not going to see an impact straight away, and it's going to be a hard slog all the way through. As long as you think that you've got the correct agencies involved, you've done the best you can do in the time you have to do it (DfES, 2005: 35)

From the perspective of a pupil support officer commenting on impact in relation to class teachers:

> Very often you only see what's going on in your class as a teacher. You only see the kids that are kicking off. You don't know that there are problems at home, you don't know any of the other business. Now the teachers know that there are other issues happening in that little person's life, that makes the biggest impact. (DfES, 2005: 39)

Leaders and managers of educational settings are accountable for the quality and reliability of the extended and multi-agency services they provide on their site. The government's ECM outcomes framework (Table 6.1), along with the National Service Framework (NSF) for children, young people and maternity services (Table 6.2)

Table 6.1 Every Child Matters outcomes

ECM outcome	ECM aims	OFSTED expectations	Government ECM targets
Be healthy	• be physically healthy • be mentally and emotionally healthy • be sexually healthy • live healthy lifestyles • choose not to take illegal drugs	• parents/carers receive support to keep children healthy • healthy lifestyles are promoted • children's physical and mental health is promoted • children are enabled and encouraged to take regular exercise • environmental health risks to children and young people are identified and minimized	• reduction in the percentage of obese children under the age of 11 • reduction in the death rate from suicide and from undetermined injury • reduction in rates of pregnancy and sexually transmitted diseases among under-18s • reduction in average alcohol consumption, harm caused by illegal drug use and the percentage of children smoking • an increase in the percentage of children eating five portions of fruit and vegetables a day
Be safe	Protect children from: • maltreatment, neglect, violence and sexual exploitation • accidental injury and death • bullying and discrimination • crime and antisocial behaviour in and out of school, and • that children should have security, stability and be cared for	• children being informed about key risks to their safety and how to deal with them • pupils in a safe environment • the incidence of child abuse and neglect minimized • local services establish the identity and whereabouts of all children aged 0 to 16 • agencies collaborate to safeguard children according to the requirements of guidance	A reduction in the: • percentage of 11–15-year-olds who have been bullied in the past year • numbers of 0–15-year-olds injured or killed in traffic accidents • re-registrations on the Child Protection Register • fear of crime and antisocial behaviour

(Continued)

Table 6.1 (Continued)

ECM outcome	ECM aims	OFSTED expectations	Government ECM targets
Enjoy and achieve	• children are ready for school • they attend and enjoy school • they achieve stretching national educational standards • they achieve personal and social development and enjoy recreation	• parents/carers receive support to help their children enjoy and achieve • action is taken to ensure that educational provision for 5- to 16-year-olds is good • educational provision is available for children who do not attend school • children have access to a range of recreational activities • Looked-after children, and those with LDD are being helped to enjoy and achieve	• percentage of 11-year-olds gaining level 4 in English and Maths • percentage of 14-year-olds meeting level 5 targets in English, Maths, Science and ICT • percentage of 16-year-olds getting five A*–C grades at GCSE, including English and Maths • half-day absences • take-up of cultural and sporting opportunities by 5- to 18-year-olds
Make a positive contribution	• engage in decision-making and support the community and the environment • engage in law-abiding and positive behaviour in and out of school • develop positive relationships and choose not to bully or discriminate • develop self-confidence and successfully deal with significant life changes and challenges • develop enterprising behaviour	The school should ensure children and young people: • are supported in developing socially and emotionally • are supported in managing changes and responding to challenges in their lives • are encouraged to participate in decision-making and in supporting the community • are encouraged to take part in and initiate voluntary activities to support the community and environment • refrain from bullying, discrimination, antisocial and criminal behaviour	• the percentage of secondary pupils participating in school council elections, mock elections, voluntary and community engagement • the percentage of 10- to 19-year-olds admitting to either bullying in the past year or threatening, attacking or being rude because of skin colour, race or religion • the number of crimes brought to justice and the number of permanent and fixed period exclusions

Table 6.1 (Continued)

ECM outcome	ECM aims	OFSTED expectations	Government ECM targets
Achieve economic well-being	• engage in further education, employment or training on leaving school • be ready for employment • live in decent homes and sustainable communities • have access to transport and material goods • live in households free of poverty	Schools: • helping to prepare 11- to 19-year-olds for working life • delivering 14–19 education in a co-ordinated way and ensuring that education and training for 16–19-year-olds is of good quality • helping looked after children and young people to achieve economic well-being • minimizing the cost of school trips for those families experiencing financial hardship • providing flexible choices that children and young people can review and revise	• the percentage of 16- to 18-year-olds not in education, employment and training (NEET) • the numbers of 18- to 30-year-olds participating in higher education • the amount of good-quality social housing • cleaner, safer and greener public spaces and the improved quality of the built environment in deprived areas • the stock and take-up of childcare for all families

Source: TES, 2008

Table 6.2 National Service Framework for children, young people and maternity services

Standard title	Standard descriptor	Main themes in standard
1. Promoting health and well-being, identifying needs and intervening early	The health and well-being of all children and young people is promoted and delivered through a co-ordinated programme of action, including prevention and early intervention wherever possible, to ensure long-term gain led by the NHS in partnership with local authorities	Child Health Programme to reduce health inequalities Multi-agency health promotion Healthy lifestyles promoted Universal and targeted health promotion Access to targeted services Early intervention and assessing needs
2. Supporting parenting	Parents and carers are enabled to receive the information, services and support which will help them to care for their children and equip them with the skills they need to ensure that their children have optimum life-chances and are healthy and safe	Universal, targeted and specialist services to support mothers and fathers Up-to-date information and education for parents Support for parents of pre-school children to help children develop secure attachments and to develop Support for parents of school-aged children to involve them in their child's learning and behaviour management Early, multi-agency support for parents with specific needs, i.e. mental health problems, addiction to drugs, alcohol; parents of disabled children, teenage parents Co-ordinated services across child and adult services Multidisciplinary support to meet the needs of adoptive parents/adults caring for looked-after children
3. Child, young person and family-centred services	Children and young people and families receive high-quality services which are co-ordinated around their individual and family needs and take account of their views	Appropriate information to children, young people and their parents Listening and responding to them in relation to their care and treatment Services respectful to the wishes of children and young people Improved access to services Robust multi-agency planning and commissioning arrangements, i.e. Children's Trusts, Common Assessment Framework Quality and safety of care in delivering of child-centred services

Table 6.2 (Continued)

Standard title	Standard descriptor	Main themes in standard
		Common core of skills, knowledge and competencies for staff working with children and young people, across all agencies
4. Growing up into adulthood	All young people have access to age-appropriate services which are responsive to their specific needs as they grow into adulthood	Confidentiality and consent for young people Health promotion to meet needs, i.e. reduce teenage pregnancy, smoking, substance misuse, suicide, sexually transmitted infections Support achievement of full potential, e.g. Connexions and Youth Services Improved access to services and advice for those who are disabled, in special circumstances or who live in rural areas Transition to full adult services Additional support available for looked-after children leaving care and other young people in special circumstances
5. Safeguarding and promoting the welfare of children and young people	All agencies work to prevent children suffering harm and to promote their welfare, provide them with the services they require to address their identified needs and safeguard children who are being or who are likely to be harmed	All agencies prioritize safeguarding and promoting the welfare of children LA children and Young People's Plan Clarification of agencies' roles and responsibilities Profile of local population to identify and assess vulnerable children High-quality integrated services to meet needs of children at risk of harm, abused or neglected Effective supervision for staff working with children to ensure clear, accurate, comprehensive, up-to-date records are kept, and high-quality services delivered
6. Children and young people who are ill	All children and young people who are ill or thought to be ill or injured will have timely access to appropriate advice and to effective services which address their health, social, educational and emotional needs throughout the period of their illness	Comprehensive, integrated, timely local services Professionals support children, young people and their families in self-care of their illness Access to advice and services in a range of settings Trained, competent professionals providing consistent advice to assist and treat a child who is ill High-quality treatment, and high-quality care for those with long-term conditions Prevention, assessment and treatment of

(Continued)

Table 6.2   (Continued)

Standard title	Standard descriptor	Main themes in standard
		pain management improved. Integrated Children's Community teams and Community Children's nursing services working outside hospital
7. Children and young people in hospital	Children and young people receive high-quality, evidence-based hospital care, developed through clinical governance and delivered in appropriate settings	Care integrated and co-ordinated around their needs. Play for children in hospital is essential Children, young people and their families treated with respect, involved in decision-making about their care, and given choices Planned discharge from hospital for children Hospital stay kept to a minimum High-quality evidence-based care provided Hospitals meet responsibilities to safeguard and promote welfare of children Care is provided in an appropriate location and in a safe environment
8. Disabled children and young people and those with complex health needs	Children and young people who are disabled or who have complex health needs, receive co-ordinated, high-quality child and family-centred services which are based on assessed needs, which promote social inclusion and, where possible, enable them and their families to live ordinary lives	Services promote social inclusion Increased access to hospital and primary health care services, therapy and equipment services, and social services Early identification of health conditions, impairments and physical barriers to inclusion through integrated diagnosis and assessment processes Early intervention and support to parents Palliative care is available where needed Services have robust systems to safeguard disabled children and young people Multi-agency transition planning occurs to support adulthood
9. The mental health and psychological well-being of children and young people	All children and young people, from birth to their eighteenth birthday, who have mental health problems and disorders have access to timely, integrated, high-quality multidisciplinary mental health services to ensure effective assessment, treatment and support, for them and their families	Professional support for children's mental health is available in the early years Staff working with children and young people contribute to early intervention and mental health promotion and develop good partnerships with children Improved access to CAMHS with high-quality multi-disciplinary CAMHS teams working in a range of settings Gaps in service addressed particularly for those with learning disabilities Care Networks developed and care in appropriate and safe settings

Table 6.2   (Continued)

Standard title	Standard descriptor	Main themes in standard
10. Medicines for children and young people	Children, young people, their parents or carers, and health care professionals in all settings make decisions about medicines based on sound information about risk and benefit. They have access to safe and effective medicines that are prescribed on the basis of the best available evidence	Safe medication practice Use of unlicensed and off-label medicines comply with local and safety standards Enhanced decision support for prescribers Improved access to medicines Clear, understandable, up-to-date information provided on medicines to users and parents. Greater support for those taking medication at home, in care and in education settings – safe storage, supply and administration of medicines Equitable access to medicines and to safeguard children in special circumstances, disabled children and those with mental health disorders Pharmacists' expertise is fully utilized
11. Maternity services	Women have easy access to supportive, high-quality maternity services, designed around their individual needs and those of their babies	Women-centred care with easy access to information and support Care pathways and managed care networks Improved pre-conception care and access to a midwife as first point of contact Local perinatal psychiatric services available Choice of where best to give birth, i.e. home or maternity unit Post-birth care provided based on a structured assessment Breastfeeding information and support for mothers

Source: DfES/DH, 2004c

enable schools leaders and heads of children's centres and PRUs to assess and evaluate collaborative activity from external multi-agency service providers. Both these frameworks also provide a common point of reference with which to track progress.

The imperative of any multi-agency partnership working is better outcomes are achieved through collective efforts. Outcomes in the context of multi-agency partnership working can therefore be defined as being the impact, effect or consequence of help received by children and young people.

The National Audit Office in 2001, outlined the minimum requirements for sound accountability in relation to multi-agency partnerships. These were:

- achieving a clear definition of the roles and responsibilities of each organization involved in the multi-agency partnership

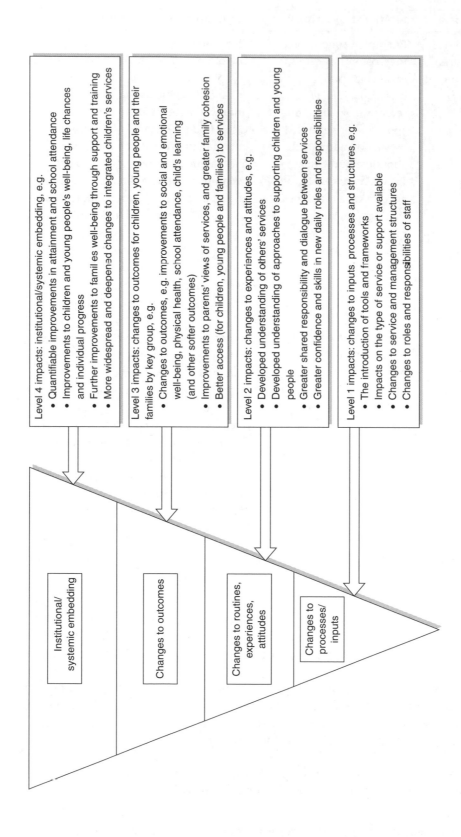

Figure 6.1   The NFER impact model

Source: Lord, Kinder, Wilkin, Atkinson and Harland, 2008: 3

Table 6.3   Examples of evaluation data used by BEST practitioners

Quantitative data	Qualitative data
• Pre- and post-intervention questionnaires • Attendance figures • Exclusion data (number and length) • Number of behaviour incidents • Attainment levels (SATs results)	• Pre- and post-intervention questionnaires • Action planning and review meetings • Practitioner case notes and observations • Pupil and school staff evaluations • Head teacher surveys • Informal feedback from pupils, parents and school staff

Source: DfES, 2005: 28

- setting out unambiguous and realistic targets for service delivery

- setting out a party responsible for taking action if progress is unsatisfactory

- reviewing and evaluating multi-agency partnerships as they evolve.

Evaluation of multi-agency provision should combine quantitative and qualitative approaches. Such approaches are essential to explaining the relative success or otherwise of the multi-agency activity/service provided. Table 6.3 provides an example of quantitative and qualitative measures for the evaluation of the BEST initiative, which is a good example of multi-agency partnership working.

OFSTED inspecting multi-agency/extended service provision

The Office for Standards in Education, during the inspection of schools and children's centres, will explore:

- why the setting has decided to offer the extended services/multi-agency provision

- how the setting's multi-agency/extended service provision is impacting on standards and achievement

- how the setting's multi-agency/extended service provision is improving the five Every Child Matters outcomes for children and young people

- how well the multi-agency/extended services activities/provision are being used.

Table 6.4 provides a useful framework for mapping and evaluating your multi-agency provision, to support the evidence gathering process for the OFSTED self-evaluation form.

Table 6.4 Mapping and evaluating the impact of multi-agency provision

ECM outcome/impact	Health	Social care	Education	Police	Voluntary and community organizations	Other agencies (Connexions, Housing)
Be healthy						
Stay safe						
Enjoy and achieve						
Positive contribution						
Economic well-being						
Impact and outcomes						
Improvement plan priorities						

Photocopiable:

In 2008 OFSTED, in their report on the impact of children's centres and extended schools, identified that leaders of these settings need to monitor and evaluate the impact of services on the achievement and attainment of children and young people, more thoroughly.

A quick self-evaluation of multi-agency partnership working

- What is working well within integrated approaches/multi-agency partnership working?

- Why do you feel it is working well?

- What has not worked as well?

- What are the views on why it has worked less well?

- What could the educational setting/children's centre do to promote, facilitate and drive better integrated multi-agency working approaches?

- How will you know if your partnership working is making a difference?

You can also utilize the evaluation framework illustrated in Figure 6.2 to evaluate how a multi-agency team is doing. It is based on four perspectives: external processes, resources, partnership management and impact. Each perspective has appropriate quantitative and/or qualitative performance indicators which are unique to the particular multi-agency partnership.

Thorlby and Hutchinson proposed a simple framework for evaluating multi-agency partnerships using four key dimensions:

1. **Rationale:** Do the multi-agency partnership's vision and aims match the needs identified? Is the programme of intervention and support appropriately targeted? Are conditions and contexts changing, and if so, is there a need for the intervention and support programme to change?

2. **Effectiveness:** What outputs have been delivered? How do they compare with the multi-agency partnerships aims and objectives? How effective has the partnership been?

3. **Cost-effectiveness:** Compare inputs and outputs. What are the unit costs? Does this represent value for money?

4. **Impact and significance:** Who is benefiting and how? What is the nature and extent of the impact and how does this compare with local conditions? What difference has the programme of intervention and support made? (Thorlby and Hutchinson, 2002: 56)

Table 6.5 Evaluating the ECM outcomes in a children's centre

Relevant PI results	Be healthy	Comments
National PIs: Local PIs:	Please set out the key activities the children's centre has undertaken to help children and families to be healthy and adopt healthy lifestyles and give an assessment of their impact. Factors to consider are: – children's and families' starting points when first making contact with the children's centre – do children take adequate physical exercise and eat and drink healthily? – what measures do you take to assess children's health and what has this shown you? – in what ways do you use good and innovative practice to improve outcomes? – are there any mitigating factors which have prevented you reading the outcomes you wanted? – what is the centre's impact on groups who find services hard to reach?	
	Overall effectiveness in meeting this outcome (rate as outstanding, good, satisfactory or inadequate)	

(Continued)

Table 6.5 (Continued)

Relevant PI results	Stay safe	Comments
National PIs:	Please set out key activities the children's centre has undertaken to help children and families to stay safe and give an assessment of their impact.	
Local PIs:	Factors to consider are:	
	– children's and families' starting points when first making contact with the children's centre	
	– how do you encourage children and their families to adopt safe practices?	
	– what measures do you take to assess children's safety and what has this shown you?	
	– in what ways do you use good and innovative practice to improve outcomes?	
	– are there any mitigating factors which have prevented you reaching the outcomes you wanted?	
	– what is the centre's impact on groups who find services hard to reach?	
	Overall effectiveness in meeting this outcome (rate as outstanding, good, satisfactory or inadequate)	

(Continued)

Table 6.5 (Continued)

Relevant PI results	Enjoy and achieve	Comments
National PIs: Local PIs:	Please set out the key activities the children's centre has undertaken to help children and families to enjoy and achieve and give an assessment of their impact. Factors to consider are: – children's and families' starting points when first making contact with the children's centre – what measures do you take to assess children's enjoyment and achievement and what has this shown you? – what are children's attitudes, behaviour and attendance? – how do you encourage children's spiritual, moral, emotional and cultural development? – in what ways do you use good and innovative practice to improve outcomes? – are there any mitigating factors which have prevented you reaching the outcomes you wanted? – what is the centre's impact on groups who find services hard to reach? **Overall effectiveness in meeting this outcome** (rate as outstanding, good, satisfactory or inadequate)	

(Continued)

Table 6.5 (Continued)

Relevant PI results	Make a positive contribution	Comments
National PIs: Local PIs:	Please set out the key activities the children's centre has undertaken to help children and families to make a positive contribution to the community and give an assessment of their impact. Factors to consider are: – children's and families' starting points when first making contact with the children's centre – what measures do you take to assess the contributions children and their families make and what has this shown you? – how do you encourage children to express their views and contribute to activities in the centre, their local community or their family? – in what ways do you use good and innovative practice to improve outcomes? – are there any mitigating factors which have prevented you reaching the outcomes you wanted? – what is the centre's impact on groups who find services hard to reach?	
	Overall effectiveness in meeting this outcome (rate as outstanding, good, satisfactory or inadequate)	

(Continued)

Table 6.5 (Continued)

Relevant PI results	Achieve economic well-being	Comments
National PIs: Local PIs:	Please set out the key activities the children's centre has undertaken to help children and families achieve economic well-being and give an assessment of their impact. Factors to consider are: – children's and families' starting points when first making contact with the children's centre – what measures do you take to assess the progress children and their families make towards achieving economic well-being and what has this shown you? – how do you link with learning providers, such as FE colleges and the local LSC and how do they link with local childcare provision? – in what ways do you use good and innovative practice to improve outcomes? – are there any mitigating factors which have prevented you reaching the outcomes you wanted? – what is the centre's impact on groups who find services hard to reach?	
	Overall effectiveness in meeting this outcome (rate as outstanding, good, satisfactory or inadequate)	

Source: Sure Start, 2007: 13–18 DfES, Self-Evaluation form for Sure Start Children's Centres pp. 13–18. © Crown Copyright 2007

 Photocopiable:

Effective Multi-Agency Partnerships, Sage Publications © Rita Cheminais, 2009

Table 6.6 Evaluating partnership working in a children's centre

How are you making the best use of private, voluntary and community provision when providing services?
Who are the private, voluntary or community organizations providing services within or in partnership with the centre? Are there groups that provide services to children and families in the area that you have not worked with? Are there plans to develop closer working links with these groups in the future?
What improvements have been made for families as a result of integration to links between services, e.g. the centre and specialist services, transition to school?
(Where appropriate) how successfully does the centre link work between its main site and satellite or other sites?
How are partner agencies (such as PCT and Jobcentre Plus) involved in the planning and decision making process?
Overall effectiveness of action to integrate services (please rate as outstanding, good, satisfactory or inadequate)

Source: Sure Start, 2007: 25

 Photocopiable:
Effective Multi-Agency Partnerships, Sage Publications © Rita Cheminais, 2009

Table 6.7 Example of an extended school evaluation profile on external partner agencies' collaborative working

Tick ✓ relevant boxes

	Consideration of current position				Direction of progress		
	Very strong	Strong	Weak	Very weak	Improving	Static	Deteriorating
Aims							
The extended school's aims are clearly expressed							
These aims are shared by all staff							
The aims have been developed in partnership							
Aims are owned by partner staff							
Aims are clearly understood by key target groups							
Collaborative culture							
Staff appreciate the demands of partner agencies							
Staff have a good understanding of partners' language and culture							
Staff understand the need for collaboration and are committed to it							
Colleagues from other organizations are valued							
Environment							
The environmental needs of staff from other agencies working in school are understood							
Adequate resources are provided to enable colleagues to work effectively							
Environmental constraints to collaboration have been addressed							

Source: Coleman, 2006: 58

Photocopiable:

Effective Multi-Agency Partnerships, Sage Publications © Rita Cheminais, 2009

Table 6.8 Evaluating the effectiveness of a multi-agency partnership

Partnership aspect	Evidence descriptor	Developing	Achieved
1. Purpose and Leadership	Share a common vision and purpose which is understood and accepted as important throughout the multi-agency partnership		
	Seek 'win-win' solutions		
	Willingness to do things differently		
	Consensus building and ownership of partnership plans and activities		
2. Outcomes and client focus	Always focused on results and outcomes		
	Satisfying the needs and expectations of clients/service users		
	Understand the needs, motivations and practices of service users		
	Involving users in service development		
3. Culture and communications	Promotes 'can do' values in getting things done		
	Accepts there are different ways of working		
	Open and effective communications at all levels, including the use of IT		
	Sustaining the partnership by fair sharing of risks and rewards among practitioners		
4. Learning and Innovation	Continuously seek improvements in activities and ways of working		
	Practitioners are keen and willing to learn from each other, and from elsewhere		
	Opportunities are created for practitioners to work and learn together to share ideas and experiment		
	Monitoring and evaluation are aimed at learning and performance improvement		
5. Management for partnership performance	Put in place necessary management practices and resources		
	Managing change to achieve partnership goals, i.e. progress unlikely without some change		
	Facilitating improvements in how practitioners work together		
	Acceptance of accountability for action		

Source: Educe, 2001: 2–8

 Photocopiable:

Effective Multi-Agency Partnerships, Sage Publications © Rita Cheminais, 2009

Table 6.9 Evaluating multi-agency partnership commitment and contributions

Educational setting's objective(s) and interests	How role/ contributions of practitioner has been affected	Driving forces that have influenced practitioners interest and commitment	Concerns and constraints for the practitioner	Importance of partnership to the practitioner	Benefits gained from practitioner involvement	Costs/risks of practitioner involvement

Source: www.lgpartnerships.com/resources/lead-assessing.asp

Photocopiable:

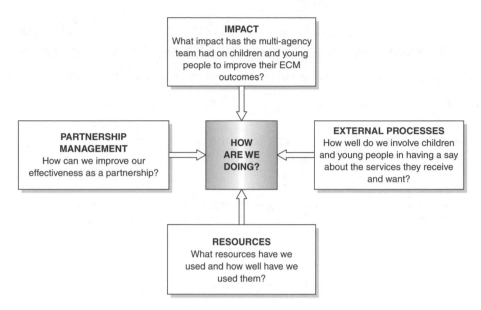

Figure 6.2   How are we doing as a multi-agency team?

What service users value most in multi-agency provision

What service users valued most in relation to services in children's centres:

- a pleasant staff manner

- ease of access to services

- a good standard of facilities

- privacy and confidentiality

- signposting and further information (DCSF, 2008a: 7).

Figure 6.4 provides a model service user survey, which can be adapted to suit the needs of the setting.

The impact of Sure Start local programmes on children and young people

The DCSF noted the following improvements:

- a reduction in crime and disorder, and fewer exclusions and unauthorized absence from schools in the area

- children aged 11 and upwards had improved academic achievement

- improvements in child health

- less economic deprivation, with fewer children living in 'workless' households (DCSF, 2008b: 26).

Figure 6.3 Multi-agency service provider survey

ANNUAL SURVEY FOR MULTI-AGENCY SERVICE PROVIDERS

Please answer the following questions to support the school's ECM evaluation.

Service: _____   Date: _____

1. How does the service you provide meet the needs of children and young people in the educational setting/children's centre?

2. How does the service you provide meet the educational setting or children's centre's aims, objectives and priorities on their improvement plan?

3. What has been the impact of the service you have delivered to children and young people in the setting?

4. How has the service been received by children, young people and their parents/carers?

5. How has the service you provided met the Every Child Matters outcomes?

6. How is the service you provided contributing to early intervention and prevention?

7. If the service you offer is chargeable, does it offer good value for money, and should the charging fee be increased?

8. Are there any services that you have offered, which you consider should not be provided in the educational setting/children's setting next year?

9. What services do you consider should be offered to children and young people in the setting, that you feel you could realistically deliver, and that would add value?

10. Have you any further comments or suggestions relating to multi-agency service provision in the setting, that you wish to make?

Thank you for taking the time to complete this survey.

Please return your survey to the Every Child Matters Co-ordinator.

 Photocopiable:

Effective Multi-Agency Partnerships, Sage Publications © Rita Cheminais, 2009

Figure 6.4   Service user survey on multi-agency provision

Annual service user survey

Please indicate who you are: Pupil ☐ Parent ☐

1. Which services have you used at the school/children's centre?

2. Have you found the services easy to access?

   Yes ☐   No ☐

   If no, state why the service(s) have not been easy to access.

3. Do you feel that the service(s) have been helpful to you in meeting your needs?

   Yes ☐   No ☐

   If no, please state how the service(s) could be improved.

4. Do you consider the service practitioners working with you listened to your views, understood your needs and respected confidentiality.

   Yes ☐   No ☐

   If no, state the reason why.

5. Do you consider the facilities and environment where you received your multi-agency service provision to be good?

   Yes ☐   No ☐

   If no, please specify how these could be improved.

6. Is there anything else you wish to comment on in relation to multi-agency service provision in the school/children's centre.

Thank you for completing this survey.

Please return your survey to the main office.

Checklist for monitoring and evaluating multi-agency provision

☐   You have built in the monitoring and evaluation of multi-agency collaboration, on the impact of service delivery, from the start.

☐   You have ensured everyone involved understands the monitoring and evaluation process being utilized.

☐   There is a named person in the setting responsible for monitoring and evaluating the impact and outcomes of multi-agency provision.

☐   There are robust procedures in place for systematically recording what is to be evaluated.

☐   Clear, agreed, shared realistic objectives are used for monitoring and evaluating impact and outcomes of multi-agency provision.

☐   You are involving an external evaluator in the process to present an objective view.

☐   You are monitoring and evaluating the effectiveness of partnership working, in addition to multi-agency service outcomes.

☐   All relevant key stakeholders are involved in the evaluation process.

☐   There is an agreed and known timescale for reporting back on outcomes.

☐   There are clear systems in place for feeding back the results from monitoring and evaluating multi-agency service provision throughout the year, and at the end, which are in an accessible form.

☐   There are clear plans and procedures in place for celebrating achievements from multi-agency service activities, within the educational setting.

Figure 6.5   Checklist for monitoring and evaluating multi-agency provision

Points to remember

- Evaluate the effectiveness of the multi-agency partnership, as well as the impact of multi-agency provision on the outcomes for children and young people.
- Ensure that your evaluation of multi-agency provision utilizes the NSF and the ECM outcomes framework, and that it feeds into the OFSTED SEF.
- Engage service users and service providers in the evaluation of multi-agency provision, along with other key stakeholders.
- Disseminate the outcomes of multi-agency evaluation to stakeholders and other interested parties, in an accessible format

Further activities

The following questions, based on aspects covered in this chapter, are designed to enable managers and members of the multi-agency team, working in the educational setting/children's centre, to identify aspects of monitoring and evaluating their service provision that requires further development and improvement.

- How do you know that the greater collaboration between multi-agency services has helped to produce better outcomes for children and young people in the educational setting/children's centre?

- How far can the improved ECM outcomes for children/young people be contributed to multi-agency collaborative partnership working?

- How are multi-agency partnerships enhancing the educational, cultural, social and leisure functions of the setting?

- How does the setting work with key partners/multi-agency practitioners to keep its community's needs, facilities and partnerships under continuous review?

- How has front-line practitioners' capacity to learn been improved and enhanced by multi-agency collaborative partnership working?

- Have there been any power relationship difficulties between multi-agency practitioners that have affected outcomes?

- What does the multi-agency team need to do differently to achieve greater collaborative advantage?

- What have been the advantages to the setting, senior management team and teachers of multi-agency involvement with vulnerable, 'at risk' children and young people?

- What have you identified as the key monitoring and evaluation priorities for your multi-agency partnership?

- How do your arrangements for monitoring and evaluating multi-agency service provision, distinguish between the output of the multi-agency partnership work it does, and the effectiveness of partnership working?

- In the context of your setting, how well are you doing overall, in relation to multi-agency partnership working?

- What key issues do you need to address in order to improve the performance and effectiveness of the multi-agency partnership in your setting?

- How do you intend disseminating the results of your monitoring and evaluation of multi-agency service outcomes to stakeholders?

- How could you further improve your quality assurance process of multi-agency working, in order to demonstrate added value?

Further information

The following websites have downloadable resources, which can help to support the monitoring and evaluation of multi-agency service provision and partnerships, within an educational setting or children's centre.

www.lgpartnerships.com   This Smarter Partnerships website has a range of self-assessment tools, which can be downloaded. They are particularly useful for reviewing partnership working in general, and in identifying trends, strengths, weaknesses and opportunities.

www.continyou.org.uk   This website has a valuable downloadable document entitled *Working in Partnership to Support Families*. Section E3 provides a useful monitoring and evaluation audit for multi-agency partnership working.

www.everychildmatters.gov.uk/deliveringservices/multiagencyworking/   This government website provides general information about monitoring and evaluating multi-agency working, which is useful for strategic leaders and managers in local authorities and educational settings/children's centres.

http://publications.teachernet.gov.uk/default.aspx?PageFunction=productdetails&PageMode=publications&ProductId=DFES-2063-2005&   This website enables you to download the ECM outcomes framework.

www.dh.gov.uk/en/Healthcare/NationalServiceFrameworks/Children/DH_4089111   This website enables you to download the National Service Framework for children, young people and maternity services. It also provides useful exemplars of applying the NSF to educational settings.

www.surestart.gov.uk/publications/?Document 1852   This website provides a downloadable version of the self-evaluation form for Sure Start children's centres, which is closely aligned to the OFSTED self-evaluation form for maintained nursery schools.

Do not forget to also visit the Sage website (www.sagepub.co.uk/cheminais) for downloadable resources to use with this chapter.

Acronyms and Abbreviations

AST	advanced skills teacher
BEST	Behaviour and Education Support Team
BSF	Building Schools for the Future
CAF	Common Assessment Framework
CAMHS	Child and Adolescent Mental Health Services
CEDC	Community Education Development Centre
CfBT	Centre for British Teachers
CLL	communication, language and literacy
CPD	continuing professional development
CRB	Criminal Records Bureau
CWDC	Children's Workforce Development Council
DCSF	Department for Children, Schools and Families
DfES	Department for Education and Skills
DH	Department of Health
ECM	Every Child Matters
ES	extended school
EWO	education welfare officer
FE	further education
FSES	full service extended school
FSP	Foundation Stage Profile
GP	general practitioner
GSCC	General Social Care Council
GTC	General Teaching Council
ICT	information and communication technology
INSET	in-service education and training
IT	information technology
LA	local authority
LAC	looked after children
LDD	learning difficulties and disabilities
LGNTO	local government national training organization
LSC	Learning and Skills Council
NCSL	National College for School Leadership
NEET	not in education, employment and training
NFER	National Foundation for Educational Research
NGfL	National Grid for Learning
NHS	National Health Service
NMC	Nursing and Midwifery Council
NOS	National Occupational Standards
NQT	newly qualified teacher
NRT	National Remodelling Team
NSF	National Service Framework
NUT	National Union of Teachers
OFSTED	Office for Standards in Education, Children's Services and Skills
PCT	primary care trust
PI	Performance Indicator

PRU	pupil referral unit
PSA	parent support adviser
PSED	Personal, Social and Emotional Development
PSHE	Personal, Social and Health Education
QTS	Qualified Teacher Status
SEF	self-evaluation form
SEN	special educational needs
SENCO	special educational needs co-ordinator
SIP	School Improvement Partner
SLT	senior leadership team
TA	teaching assistant
TAC	Team Around the Child
TDA	Training and Development Agency for Schools
TES	Times Educational Supplement
TFC	Together for Children
VCS	voluntary community sector
YOT	Youth Offending Team

Glossary

Agency – a statutory or voluntary organization, where staff are paid or unpaid, work with or have access to children, young people and families.

Change – is a process designed to improve practice, introduce new policies and functions and alter the existing practice.

Children's centre – a one-stop shop and community service hub for parents/carers and children under 5, offering early education and childcare, family support, health services, employment advice and specialist support on a single site, to improve their life chances.

Children's trusts – help to bring together schools with specialist support services, voluntary community sector providers, who can help; they broker imaginative solutions to provision.

Collaboration – a process of working jointly with others, including those with whom one is not normally or immediately connected, to develop and achieve common goals.

Colleagues – all those professionals with whom a teacher may have a professional working relationship with. They may include teaching colleagues, teaching assistants, and the wider children's workforce from education, health and social care working with teachers within an educational setting.

Commissioning – the process of defining priorities, and determining how services are delivered, particularly by allocating resources differently, in order to achieve better outcomes and results for children, young people and their families.

Common Assessment Framework – a holistic assessment process used by professionals and practitioners in the children's workforce to assess the additional needs of children and young people at the first signs of difficulties.

ContactPoint – a quick way to find out who else is working with the same child or young person, making it easier to deliver more co-ordinated support.

Extended school – a school that provides a range of core universal services and activities, often beyond the school day, to help meet the needs of its pupils, their families and the wider community.

Federation – a group of two or more schools, with a formal agreement to work together to raise standards. They may share services.

Information sharing – the process of passing on relevant information to other agencies, organizations and individuals that require it, in order to deliver better services to children and young people.

Inter-agency working – when more than one agency work together in a planned and formal way.

Integrated working – when agencies work together within a single, often new, organizational structure.

Joint working – when professionals from more than one agency work directly together on a project.

Lead professional – a designated professional (usually from health, social care or education services), who has day-to-day contact with a child or young person, and who co-ordinates and monitors service provision, acting as a gatekeeper for information sharing.

Multi-agency managed model of leadership – a model of leadership that entails a greater degree of multi-agency working, and a more diverse children's workforce, being based in the educational setting. A school's senior leadership team is likely to have representatives from the multi-agency services on it, in this type of leadership model.

Multi-agency working – where those from more than one agency or service work together jointly, sharing aims, information, tasks and responsibilities.

Multi-agency/cross-agency working – when a number of services provided by agencies, act in concert, and draw on pooled resources or pooled budgets.

National Service Framework – a set of quality standards for health, social care and some education services, and is aimed at reducing inequalities in service provision in order to improve the lives and health of children and young people.

Outcomes – the identifiable (positive or negative) impact of interventions, programmes or services on children and young people.

Partnership – where two or more people or organizations work together towards a common aim.

Practitioner – anyone who works directly with children, young people and their families, whose primary role is to use a particular expertise or professional skill in order to help promote children and young people's well-being.

Stakeholder – any person, group, organization or institution that has an interest in an activity, project, initiative or development. This includes intended beneficiaries and intermediaries, winners and losers and those involved or excluded from the decision-making process.

Team Around the Child – an individualized, personalized and evolving team of a few different practitioners, who come together to provide practical support to help an individual child.

Vulnerable children – those children and young people who are at risk of social exclusion, those who are disadvantaged and whose life chances are likely to be jeopardized unless action is taken to better meet their needs. This includes those in public care, children with learning difficulties and disabilities, travellers, asylum seekers, excluded pupils, truants, young offenders, young family carers, children living in families experiencing stress and children affected by domestic violence.

Well-being – having the basic things you need to live and be healthy, safe and happy. Every Child Matters has five well-being outcomes: be healthy, stay safe, enjoy and achieve, make a positive contribution and achieve economic well-being.

Young person – someone who is under the age of 18, that is, aged between 14 and 17.

Further Reading and References

Arnstein, S.R. (1969) 'A Ladder of Citizen Participation', *Journal of the American Planning Association*, 35(4) July: 216–24.

Atkinson, M., Wilkin, A., Stott, A. and Kinder, K. (2001) *Multi-Agency Working: An Audit of Activity*. LGA research report 17. Slough: NFER.

Atkinson, M., Wilkin, A., Stott, A., Doherty, P. and Kinder, K. (2002) *Multi-Agency Working: A Detailed Study*. LGA Research Report No. 26. Slough: NFER.

Atkinson, M., Jones, M. and Lamont, E. (2007) *Multi-Agency Working and Its Implications for Practice: A Review of the Literature*. Reading: CfBT.

Blair, T. (1997) *Bringing Britain Together*. Speech by the Prime Minister, The Rt. Hon. Tony Blair MP. Stockwell Park School, South London. 8 December 1997.

Brown, K. and White, K. (2006) *Exploring the Evidence Base for Integrated Children's Services*. Edinburgh: Scottish Executive Education Department.

Cambridgeshire County Council (2006) *Good Practice Examples in Cambridgeshire*. Cambridge: Children and Young People's Services.

CEDC/ContinYou (2003) *Parentaid: A 'How to' Guide*. London: Community Education Development Centre and ContinYou.

CfBT (2007) *Schools as community Based Organisations*. Reading: Centre for British Teachers Education Trust.

Cheminais, R. (2007) *Extended Schools and Children's Centres. A Practical Guide*. London: Routledge.

Children's Rights Alliance for England (2005) *Ready Steady Change. Participation Training Handbook – Adults*. London: Children's Rights Alliance for England.

Coleman, A. (2006) *Collaborative Leadership in Extended Schools. Leading in a Multi-Agency Environment*. Nottingham: National College for School Leadership.

ContinYou (2005a) *How are we doing? A Self-Evaluation Toolkit for Extended Schools. The Framework*. London: ContinYou.

ContinYou (2005b) *Working in Partnership to Support Families. Flexible Materials*. London: ContinYou.

Craig, J., Huber, J. and Lownsbrough, H. (2004) *Schools Out. Can Teachers, Social Workers and Health Staff Learn to Live Together*. London: DEMOS/Hay Group Education.

CWDC (2007) *Multi-Agency Working. Fact Sheet*. London: Children's Workforce Development Council.

CWDC/TFC (2007) *Children's Centres: an Integrated Workforce in Practice. Cameos of Practice in East of England*. London: Children's Workforce Development Council and Together for Children.

DCSF (2007a) *Integrated Working Exemplar: Young Child with Behavioural Problems. Integrated Working to Improve Outcomes for Children and Young People*. London: Department for Children, Schools and Families.

DCSF (2007b) *Integrated Working Exemplar: Bright Teenager with Truancy and Transition Issues. Integrated Working to Improve Outcomes for Children and Young People*. London: Department for Children, Schools and Families.

DCSF (2007c) *Integrated Working Exemplar: Troubled Young Person. Integrated Working to Improve Outcomes for Children and Young People*. London: Department for Children, Schools and Families.

DCSF (2008a) *Sure Start Children's Centres: Building Brighter Futures*. Nottingham: Department for Children, Schools and Families.

DCSF (2008b) *The Sure Start Journey – A Summary of Evidence*. Nottingham: Department for Children, Schools and Families.

DfES (2002) *Extended Schools Providing Opportunities and Services for All*. London: Department for Education and Skills.

DfES (2003) *Every Child Matters*. Norwich: The Stationery Office.

DfES (2004a) *Every Child Matters: Change for Children*. Nottingham: Department for Education and Skills.

DfES (2004b) *Every Child Matters: Change for Children in Schools*. Nottingham: Department for Education and Skills.

DfES (2005) *Evaluation of Behaviour and Education Support Teams*. Nottingham: Department for Education and Skills/NFER.

DfES (2006) *Making it Happen. Working Together for Children, Young People and Families*. London: Department for Education and Skills.

DfES (2007) *Independent Study into School Leadership. Main Report*. London: PriceWaterhouseCoopers LLP.

DfES/DH (2004c) *National Service Framework for Children, Young People and Maternity Services*. London: Department for Education and Skills.

DH (2002) *Keys to Partnership. Working Together to Make a Difference to People's lives*. London: Department of Health.

Educe (2001) *Five Vital Lessons. High Performing Partnerships*. http://fivevital.educe.co.uk/index_1.htm (accessed 10 March 2008).

Gaster, L., Deakin, N., Riseborough, M., McCabe, A., Wainwright, S. and Rogers, H. (1998) *History, Strategy or Lottery? The Realities of Local Government/Voluntary Sector Relationships*. Birmingham: Local Government Management Board and the University of Birmingham.

GTC (2007) *Joint Statement of Inter-professional Values Underpinning Work with Children and Young People*. London: General Teaching Council.

GTC (2007a) *HM Government: Children's Workforce Strategy Update – Spring 2007. Building a World-Class Workforce for Children, Young People and Families*. London: General Teaching Council.

GTC (2007b) *Inter-professional Values Underpinning Work with Children and Young People Joint Statement*. London: General Teaching Council for England.

Harris, A., Allen, T. and Goodall, J. (2007) *Understanding the Reasons Why Schools Do or Do Not Fully Engage with the ECM/ES Agenda*. Nottingham: National College for School Leadership and the Training and Development Agency for Schools.

Her Majesty's Government (2005) *Common Core of Skills and Knowledge for the Children's Workforce*. London: Department for Education and Skills.

Her Majesty's Government (2007) *Children's Workforce Strategy. Building a World-Class Workforce for Children, Young People and Families*. London: Department for Education and Skills.

Huxham, C. and Vangen, S. (2005) *Managing to Collaborate: The Theory and Practice of Collaborative Advantage*. Abingdon: Routledge.

Jones, J. (2006) *Children and Young People's Views about 'Team Around the Child'. How You Have Helped Make a Difference*. Leicester: Mindful Practice Limited, Shropshire County Council and Telford and Wrekin Council.

Joseph Rowntree Foundation (1998) *Housing officers and Multi-Agency Work with Children and Young People on Social Housing Estates*. York: Chartered Institute of Housing in association with Joseph Rowntree Foundation.

Kendall, S., Lamont, E., Wilkin, A. and Kinder, K. (2007) *Every Child Matters. How School Leaders in Extended Schools Respond to Local Needs*. Nottingham: National College for School Leadership/NFER.

Limbrick, P. (2001) *The Team Around The Child: Multi-agency service co-ordination for children with complex needs and their families*. Worcester. Interconnections.

Limbrick, P. (2005) *Principles and Practice that Define the Team-Around-the-Child (TAC) Approach and their Relationship to Accepted Good Practice*. Worcester: Interconnections.

Limbrick, P. (2007) *The Foundations of the Team Around the Child (TAC) Model*. Worcester: Interconnections.

Lord, P., Kinder, K., Wilkin, A., Atkinson, M. and Harland, J. (2008) *Evaluating the Early Impact of Integrated Children's Services: Round 1 Summary Report*. Slough: NFER.

McInnes, K. (2007) *A Practitioner's Guide to Interagency Working in Children's Centres: A Review of the Literature*. Barkingside: Barnardo's Policy and Research Unit.

Moran, P., Jacobs, C., Bunn, A. and Bifulco, A. (2007) 'Multi-agency working: implications for an early-intervention social work team', *Child and Family Social Work*, 12: 143–51.

NASEN (2004) *Draft Policy Document on Partnership Working*. Tamworth: National Association of Special Educational Needs.

National Audit Office (2001) *Joining Up to Improve Public Services*. London: National Audit Office.

National Audit Office (2006) *Sure Start Children's Centres*. London: The Stationery Office.

NCSL (2008) *What Are We Learning About: Leadership of Every Child Matters*. Nottingham: National College for School Leadership.

NFER (2006) *How Is the Every Child Matters Agenda Affecting Schools? Annual Survey of Trends in Education 2006*. Slough: National Foundation for Educational Research.

NFER (2007) *How Is the Every Child Matters Agenda Affecting Schools? Annual Survey of Trends in Education 2007*. Slough: National Foundation for Educational Research.

OFSTED (2008) *How Well Are They Doing? The Impact of Children's Centres and Extended Schools*. London: Office for Standards in Education, Children's Services and Skills.

OurPartnership (2007) *The Partnership Life Cycle Toolkit*. www.ourpartnership.org.uk/anncmnt/ (accessed 10 March 2008).

Paton, R. and Vangen, S. (2004) *Understanding and Developing Leadership in Multi-agency Children and Family Teams*. London: Department for Education and Skills (DfES).

Percy-Smith, J. (2005) *What Works in Strategic Partnerships for Children?* Essex: Barnardo's.

Piper, J. (2005) *From Cutty Sark to Airbus – The Potential for Extended Schools and their Communities*. PowerPoint presentation. London: The Extended Schools Support Service/ContinYou.

Sure Start (2006) *Children's Centres. Leading the Way*, newsletter, autumn: 13.

Sure Start (2007) *Self-Evaluation Form For Sure Start Children's Centres*. London: Sure Start.

TDA (2007a) *National Occupational Standards for Supporting Teaching and Learning in Schools*. London: Training and Development Agency for Schools.

TDA (2007b) *Professional Standards for Teachers. Why Sit Still in Your Career?* London: Training and Development Agency for Schools.

TDA (2007c) *School Improvement Planning Framework: Module 2c ECM Outcomes*. London: Training and Development Agency for Schools.

TES (2008) *The Big 5, Times Educational Supplement* Special Series.

TFC (2007) *Data and Information Sharing*. London: Together for Children.

TFC (2007) *Working in Partnership to Deliver Preventive Speech and Language Services*. London: Together for Children.

The Housing Corporation (2002) *The Big Picture. Young People and Housing Associations*. London: The Housing Corporation.

Thorlby, T. and Hutchinson, J. (2002) *Working in Partnership: A Sourcebook*. London: New Opportunities Fund.

Together for Children (2007) *Case Study Proforma v1*. http//www.childrens-centres. org/Topics/CaseStudies/AllCaseStudies.aspx (accessed 7 December 2007).

Tomlinson, K. (2003) *Effective Interagency Working: A Review of the Literature and Examples from Practice*. LGA Research Report 40. Slough: NFER.

Tuckman, B.W. (1965) 'Developmental sequences in small groups', *Psychological Bulletin,* 63, 384–99.

Vaughan, R., Baines, S., Martin, M. and Wilson, R. (2006) *FAME Phase 3 – Generic Framework*. Newcastle: Newcastle University.

Wilcox, D. (2000) *Creating Partnerships: Participation and Partnership – Five Stances*. www.partnerships.org.uk/AZP/part.html (accessed 17 February 2008).

Wilcox, D. (2004) *A Short Guide to Partnerships*. www.partnerships.org.uk/part (accessed 17 February 2008).

Wilkin, A., Murfield, J., Lamont, J., Kinder, K. and Dyson, P. (2008) *The Value of Social Care Professionals Working in Extended Schools*. Slough: National Foundation for Educational Research.

Index

Added to a page number 'f' denotes a figure and 't' denotes a table.